# UNFUCK YOUR
# PARENTING

## How to Raise Feminist, Compassionate, Responsible, and Generally Non-Shitty Kids

## DR. FAITH G. HARPER, ACS, ACN, & BONNIE SCOTT, MA, LPC-S

## MICROCOSM PUBLISHING
Portland, Ore | Cleveland, OH

# UNFUCK YOUR PARENTING

## How to Raise Feminist, Compassionate, Responsible, and Generally Non-Shitty Kids

© This edition Microcosm Publishing 2025
First edition – 3,000 copies – January 14, 2025
ISBN 9781648413933
This is Microcosm # 893

Edited by Olivia Rollins
Designed by Joe Biel
Cover by Lindsey Cleworth and Joe Biel

All the news that's fit to print at www.Microcosm.Pub/Newsletter
Get more copies of this book at www.Microcosm.Pub/UnfuckParenting
Find more work by Dr. Faith at www.Microcosm.Pub/DrFaithBooks

**To join the ranks of high-class stores that feature Microcosm titles, talk to your rep:** In the U.S. **COMO** (Atlantic), **ABRAHAM** (Midwest), **BOB BARNETT** (Texas, Oklahoma, Arkansas, Louisiana), **IMPRINT** (Pacific); **TURNAROUND** (UK), **UTP/MANDA** (Canada), **NEWSOUTH** (Australia/New Zealand), **Observatoire** (Africa, Europe), **IPR** (Middle East), **Yvonne Chau** (Southeast Asia), **HarperCollins** (India), **Everest/B.K. Agency** (China), **Tim Burland** (Japan/Korea), and **FAIRE** in the gift trade.

For a catalog, write or visit:

Microcosm Publishing
2752 N Williams Ave.
Portland, OR 97227
https://microcosm.pub/Parenting

Did you know that you can buy our books directly from us at sliding scale rates? Support a small, independent publisher and pay less than Amazon's price at **www.Microcosm.Pub**

*Library of Congress Cataloging-in-Publication Data*
Names: Harper, Faith G., author. | Scott, Bonnie (Counselor), author.
Title: Unfuck your parenting : how to raise feminist, compassionate,
responsible, and generally non-shitty kids / by Faith G. Harper, PhD, &
Bonnie Scott, MA, LPC-S.
Description: [Portland] : Microcosm Publishing, [2024] | Summary: "How do
you raise your kids to be functional adults with big hearts? Young
people need to learn to stand up against every kind of oppression,
respect boundaries and consent, and gain self-compassion while also
navigating money, friends, sex, and school. How can you prepare children
and teens to find joy and stability as they cope with uncertainty,
violence, and disaster, especially when your own coming-of-age lessons
weren't so thoughtfully taught? Parents and therapists Dr. Faith G.
Harper and Bonnie Scott have written a parenting guide for the 21st
century"-- Provided by publisher.
Identifiers: LCCN 2023050691 | ISBN 9781648413933 (trade paperback)
Subjects: LCSH: Child rearing. | Parenting.
Classification: LCC HQ769 .H286 2024 | DDC 649/.1--dc23/eng/20231116
LC record available at https://lccn.loc.gov/2023050691

# MICROCOSM · PUBLISHING

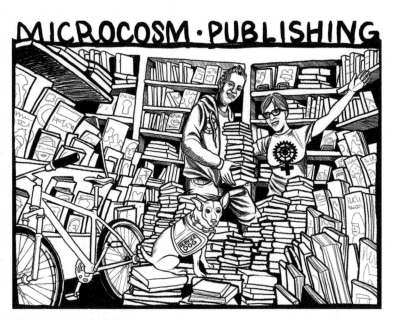

**MICROCOSM PUBLISHING** is Portland's most diversified publishing house and distributor with a focus on the colorful, authentic, and empowering. Our books and zines have put your power in your hands since 1996, equipping readers to make positive changes in their lives and in the world around them. Microcosm emphasizes skill-building, showing hidden histories, and fostering creativity through challenging conventional publishing wisdom with books and bookettes about DIY skills, food, bicycling, gender, self-care, and social justice. What was once a distro and record label was started by Joe Biel in his bedroom and has become among the oldest independent publishing houses in Portland, OR. We are a politically moderate, centrist publisher in a world that has inched to the right for the past 80 years.

Global labor conditions are bad, and our roots in industrial Cleveland in the 70s and 80s made us appreciate the need to treat workers right. Therefore, our books are MADE IN THE USA.

# CONTENTS

# INTRODUCTION

*P*arenting is a high-stakes gig. The question isn't "Will I mess this up?" but "How bad am I going to mess this up?" Because the universal truth of parenting is that parents will mess up. That realization is stressful, because when we fuck it up, are we fucking up a kid's life, and our own, for eternity? Are we doomed to repeat the fuck ups our parents made, or can we mostly avoid those and make our own unique fuck ups instead?

The already high stakes of parenting today seem higher than ever. The generation we're raising now is facing a lot of social and economic upheaval, polarized politics, increasing bias and hate, gun violence, and climate catastrophe. How do we raise them to be resilient and safe . . . and also to stand for what's right? All while still being thoughtful, kind, happy, healthy, housed, and fed. And how do we do this without losing our minds ourselves?

We're here to tell you that it won't be easy; honestly, the stuff worth doing is rarely easy. But we can work together, support one another, be nonjudgmental, and help each parent find the balance that's right for them and their family.

How does our parenting get fucked up? There's our own trauma, self-doubt, and other internal stuff for us to work on, not to mention that external bullshit that we have to teach our kids to deal with. We'll give you skills for all of that. We're going to talk about creating safe homes, teaching self-compassion, regulating stress, and building community that supports progressive parents and parenting.

Maybe you already have kids in your home or life, whether you donated genetic material to their conception or not. Or maybe you are preparing for the imminent arrival of a child or just starting to think about having kids of your own. Either way, we feel hopeful you'll find some ideas here that will be helpful to you in raising and supporting the kids around you to be thoughtful, progressive, and inclusive.

We are friends and parents and have trained and worked as professional therapists. We've also worked with hundreds of parents in-session or workshops to improve parent–kid relationships. We both work from a relational therapy framework and we know how important a healthy and supportive parenting relationship can be.

Faith is bio mom to two kids (now young adults) and bonus mom/Indigenous auntie to many more. Her youngest currently lives at their home in Texas, doing her yard work and bringing her iced coffee while establishing his career. They live alongside five rescue cats (of course, Faith's a middle-aged weirdo) and aforementioned son's cattle dog and his two new rescue kittens (the cat distribution system pours with a heavy hand in this family). Bonnie is mom to one elementary school kid, two poorly behaved cats, and one poorly behaved dog.

As adults, we are working toward a more egalitarian world; we also need to build the scaffolding for future progress and safety for all. The sturdiness of this scaffolding relies on us teaching our kids about the realities of the world and the possibilities, too.[1]

The common saying "There's no such thing as other people's kids" is a guiding principle of this book. What affects one kid affects them all in some way. The decisions that get made around health care, education, libraries, school lunch programming, sports, bathrooms . . . those affect all kids. What affects yours also affects ours and vice versa. This means we treat all kids the way we wish our own kids could be treated:

---

[1] If you're familiar with the poem "Good Bones" by Maggie Smith, that's a good encapsulation of what we're getting at here.

with kindness, thoughtfulness, and foresight. It takes all of us, looking out for all of them, to make real and lasting changes in society. So when we talk about "parenting" in the context of this book, really what we are talking about is the common denominator of guiding and caring about young people and their futures.

Maybe you're a bio parent, a stepparent, an adoptive or foster parent, a cool auntie, a youth director, a teacher, or a bus driver. Regardless, you're a person who has responsibility to and for young people. Much of the feedback we got from the first edition of this book was from people who work with kids but don't have any themselves and are using the book to be better at their jobs. And we can't begin to tell you how much we respect and admire and love you for loving our kids. Thank you.

In addition to memories of our own childhoods and our understanding of feminism and family, the ideas and topics in this book are a compilation of conversations with our own kids, their friends, our friends, our clients, and our own families. We talk about a lot of emotional stuff and we include some practical life skills as well. This book is meant to serve as a guide for parents who want to raise well-rounded kids with progressive, feminist values, and also teach kids how to act on those values to make real changes in their communities while taking care of their own basic needs. Therefore, this is an unapologetically feminist parenting book, something we've already experienced pushback about.[2] You don't have to self-identify as a "feminist" to read it and learn from it, but we aren't shying away from the values that are most important to us, and many of our examples do assume progressive values around treating all humans with respect and fighting systems of oppression.

---

2 There was a push to have the first edition of this book banned. C'mon guys, it isn't required reading. We will leave your books alone if you leave ours alone, okay?

We first started this project as a series of zines, and we wanted it to reflect the newer, more intersectional feminism rather than the one we grew up with. So we called the project Woke Parenting. In 2017, the word "woke" was added to *Merriam-Webster*, which defined it as "aware of and actively attentive to important facts and issues (especially issues of racial and social justice)." The term is much older than that, of course. It was first used in reference to political or social consciousness in a 1962 *New York Times* essay by novelist William Melvin Kelley. It started to really gain traction after Erykah Badu used "I stay woke" as a hook in her song "Master Teacher" in 2008.

Once "woke" was added to the dictionary, it became a cultural flash point. It started showing up in all kinds of different contexts, like *SNL* skits, daytime talk shows, coffee mugs and t-shirts, and the conversations of suburban teens on TikTok. The alt-right quickly latched on and took up "anti-woke" as a way to rile up supporters. They used their twisted version of wokeness to embody a new, yet familiar, disdain for progressive elitism that threatens "traditional" values, just like they've done with other movements in the past.

The word is used with contempt by politicians and conservative pundits in a way that is very much meant to make people afraid of progress. Now they've taken all the fun out of even joking about being woke, but the original use of the term still has a deep power. It may have been co-opted, but it can't be corrupted. Because woke means *we don't look away*. From any of it. Our mandate as humans is to be in and of this world. It is still meaningful to "wake up" to injustice, discrimination, or hatred and see the ways each of us can work toward the more just world we want for our kids. It is still important to do the work of seeing and responding to injustice, processing our own guilt and pain, and treating the process as sacred and necessary.

The basic principles here are straightforward, no matter what terms we're using to describe them: These ideals are woke, feminist, progressive, restorative, inclusive, equitable, and optimistic. This isn't liberalism as the antithesis of conservatism. It is progressivism in the face of facism. And it is meant to make everyone's lives better because it's rooted in a deep desire to make things right and move society forward, together. The work of justice is the important thing, so if calling it "woke" is turning people away, we need a different call.

So we changed the title.

The cranks also hate the books in the "unfuck" series, so now they have a new title to complain about while the rest of us get back to work. The work of feminism and antiracism isn't just what we say, or think, or read. It is action that fosters empathy, builds community, and moves us toward healing. We all need to be in and of this world, and raise kids that live the same. This is the only way to save us.

That makes it sound both easier and harder than it is in reality, of course. The ground shifts quickly, both in our personal lives and in the wider sphere. Over the course of writing the original zines and book, Bonnie's kid grew from a salty toddler to a salty elementary school student. Faith's kids grew all the way up and moved out to lives of their own, coming back when they needed a reboot, and it happened so quickly.

Add to that feeling of "I blinked and now all their shoes are too small" the idea of keeping up with a quickly shifting cultural experience, and wow, it can be a dizzying challenge. There's a lot to navigate between changing bodies, changing needs, changing emotions (parents' and kids'), changing climate, and changing politics. Parenting asks for our best selves, and that's all we can give in the uncertainty around us.

In this book, we're hoping to help you find some stable ground to stand on. We've made significant revisions in turning this into *Unfuck Your Parenting*. The book is still very much about how to raise kids who'll be aware and do good in the world, but we're framing it more in terms of what you need, as the parent, to be able to meet your kids' needs and raise them well while still maintaining your own sense of self and sanity.

The structure of this book starts with your internal life and choices as the parent and moves outward into the wider world.

We'll start with talking about how to take care of yourself. We are starting here because self-care is fuel for compassion and action. When you take good care of yourself, you build capacity for taking care of others. How do we make better parents if all the parents are burnt out and bitter because they didn't have the self-care skills they needed? For us to show up as the best versions of ourselves, we've got to nourish the best versions of ourselves.

From there, we will talk about how to work with the other adults in your kids' lives so your kids get consistent messaging and you get the support you need. There will be some ideas about boundaries, cultural traditions, and making more friends.

Then we'll move on to how to create a safe and supportive home environment and how to foster discussions around health and safety in ways that match your values. These conversations will be focused on things like diet culture, feeling and showing emotions, and constructive ways to give feedback.

Next, we'll move those values into your community and talk about things like race, gender, and ability, things that affect who we are as people and how we interact with other people and our environments. This section will build on the skills of self-care, accountability, and our ability to value other people's experiences.

Then we will foster some discussions about physical safety, managing bullies, and navigating sexual consent. We'll also need some tough conversations here about school violence, substance use, and existing on the internet.

We'll then take all these interpersonal skills into the wider sphere where we give some ideas on how to talk about current events, major political issues, and the future of our communities.

Finally, we will wrap it up with a list of discrete skills we can teach kids (and maybe ourselves if we missed learning them earlier!) that will help them navigate the basics of life and supplement all of their thoughtful actions toward progressive change.

See this as a guide to creating a culture of support and openness in your home and with your kids so they have a better chance of growing up to be collaborative people who can carry their own physical and emotional labor. Whether your kids are newborn, basically grown, or somewhere in between, it's never too late to start shifting your approach to them in order to support their emotional and relational growth.

Part of the privilege of parenting is the fact that it is hard as *fuck*. If we bang one drum repeatedly, it is that worthwhile work is rarely easy or able to be done on autopilot. Parenting requires presence, vulnerability, empathy, and patience. We say this because we see so many wonderful, human parenting people frustrated with themselves that this isn't one of those "once you learn how to ride a bike you will always be able to ride a bike" skills. Parenting is one of those chances to be the best that humanity has to offer.

We hope this book gives you a framework for talking about your own beliefs and values with kids in your life and helps you create a space for discussion and growth. Don't wait for your kid to get competing messages from greater society, before they've heard these ideas or had a chance to work for justice and progress.

# Square-Breathing Exercise

We're going to ask you to do hard things, have hard conversations, and also not lose your shit when your kid is being a butt. So here's something to help! And this is not only a great coping skill for you—it's also one you can teach your kids.

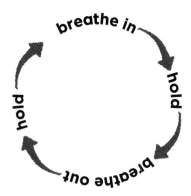

Start by just paying attention to your breathing for about a minute, and see what you notice by being mindful, without actively trying to change your breathing patterns. Are they rapid? Shallow? Are you holding your breath?

Now, try the following for at least another minute:

1. Breathe in, through your nose, counting to four slowly. Focus on feeling the air enter your lungs. You can trace the top of the box diagram from left to right to help guide you.

2. Hold your breath for another four seconds, if your lung capacity allows it. To help guide you, you can trace down the right side of the box diagram from the top point you landed on.

3. Now, slowly exhale through your mouth for another four seconds. You can trace across the bottom of the box, now going right to left.

4. Hold your breath again for another four seconds, tracing the left side of the diagram from bottom to top.

Repeat this exercise as many times as you can. Even 30 seconds of deep breathing will help you feel more relaxed and in control.

# TAKE CARE OF
# YOURSELF

*R*eal talk: parenting is more than just raising your kids right. It's about learning to be a better person yourself, too. Parenting asks us to be incredibly flexible and adaptive; that can be difficult to lean into. Here we discuss how to learn for yourself, how to be open and better at communication, and how to take good care of yourself. A kinder, more peaceful world begins with all of us being kinder and more peaceful with ourselves. This section is begging you to do some work on yourself with compassion and, hopefully, emerge feeling a bit more free from the societal messages you may have absorbed throughout life. You're not going to overcome a lifetime of conditioning quickly or easily, but you can go bravely and boldly into new spaces by asking new questions and bringing curiosity to your own experiences. Move gently into this new and vulnerable space.

There seems to be a prevailing sense in society that parenting should be "selfless" and that denying your needs, humanity, or personality for your kids is the preferable and acceptable way to parent. That's bullshit. Parenting takes balance; it takes the occasional late night with a sick kid *and* the occasional night out to the movies with a partner or friend (or by yourself because then there's no competition for popcorn). Parenting isn't a zero-sum game, no matter how many times you've seen it framed that way in popular culture or by some judgy person in the grocery line.

We get it, taking care of yourself when you have kids with bottomless needs can feel really selfish. But let's look at what it means to be selfish for a second. Being selfish in the traditional sense is a bad thing; it's egotistical, focusing primarily on your own gain or pleasure with no concern for others' needs or wellbeing. That's not what we are advocating for here. We are advocating for focusing on your needs and pleasures as a human with the end goal of being more present and open to the needs and wants of others in your life. By showing compassion toward yourself, you're making others' lives better, and that's definitely not selfish; that's in fact, the famous and elusive win-win scenario. You are being self-focused to have your needs met so you can then meet the needs of others. There is nothing shitty about that.

No one can pour from an empty cup. Parenting takes a lot of pouring. That's part of the job description when you let a child-person into your life, and we all know it. But parenting is not "pour until you've forgotten yourself and then you hate everyone and then you're grumpy and yelling again" because that doesn't work for anyone.

This section is a discussion about finding what you need to feel nurtured so you have plenty of energy and headspace to nurture others. Filling your cup is about making sure you have the available capacity to care for other people and do the relational work required to raise kids in an increasingly complex world. This act of caring for yourself means that you have a realistic idea of the energy, attention, and time available to you to meet the demands of your life. That can look different all the time, but if you're paying attention, you'll know if you have the capacity to meet the needs of today, or if you need to step back or ask for support. You're connecting with yourself, so you know what you have available to give to others.

Additionally, you're going to be modeling for your kids how it can look to have a full, energetic, exciting life where you have lots of outlets for creativity. You're raising a generation of young folks who will know that they deserve space to nurture themselves and that they can focus on many parts of life without slipping into burnout. How different could the next generation's relationship to caregiving be if they saw you setting boundaries and finding meaningful rest?

In American capitalism, any focus on self-care has been designed to *sell* said care. Capitalistic self-care isn't meant to be intuitive or to help you learn about your own capacity for meeting the demands of your day or life. This type of self-care is focused entirely on your capacity to continue to benefit capitalism, always teetering on the edge of burnout but never really getting what you want or need to feel rested. We hope the conversations here will be a spark for you to find ways to rest, connect, and make meaning for yourself and your loved ones. You deserve rest!

This is the chapter where we, two professional people with child-people of our own, give you permission to fill your cup. And we will keep giving you permission until you give *yourself* permission to get what you need, to move toward balance in your life, and to do it without guilt. Because when you're parenting from a place of contentment and forgiveness for yourself, you can give more of that attitude to your loved ones. You're more likely to be the parent you want to be if you're engaging in meaningful self-care.

Let's take some time here to assess your current feelings about rest and self-care. Consider these questions:

- What messages did you get from your caregivers about self-care?

- Have you tied your ability to provide for others to your feelings about your self-worth?

- What are your beliefs about rest?

- How are those beliefs affecting your levels of rest and capacity?

- How would your life be different if you treated taking care of yourself as a necessity?

- What needs of your own are you setting as lower priority than needs of others?

- How do you interact with your family when you are feeling rested and nurtured?

- How is that different from how you interact when you're burnt out and tired?

With your answers in mind, let's move on to identify some areas you can focus on as you leave burnout behind you and find new energy and attention for yourself.

If we are taking good care of ourselves, taking care of others becomes an act of love and can feel fulfilling and joyful. If we aren't, all that caring becomes a big ole chore, and nobody likes to feel like a chore. Faith and Bonnie both talk to a lot of clients who share with us the struggle of parenting and sometimes losing our own identities along the way. We all deserve a chance to have a quiet moment, to disconnect and disengage, to know ourselves in our own ways and not just in parent ways.

# Create a Self-Care Plan

If you answered those questions and found that your cup is feeling quite empty, start by asking yourself, "What do I need? What would feel good right now?" There are likely some relatively small, easier-to-meet needs that will come to mind. Identify one, and give it to yourself. Notice the joy that arises when our need to feel nurtured is met. Joy is our weapon against burnout and resentment. When we actively seek and feel joy, we build our capacity for activism and relationships.

Make a list of go-to things that bring down your stress levels and help you feel cared for. This list is your first stop on this self-love tour. We are asking you to spend some time with yourself, assess your needs, and start thinking of accessible ways to address those needs. Maybe it's a few deep breaths and stretching, or a lovely cup of tea, or a few rounds with the punching bag. Maybe you review your calendar and identify one thing you can let go of or delegate this week. Step outside and feel the sun on your skin. Organize a bathroom drawer. Connect with a person or pet who loves you. This list is yours, and it is unique and important.

Keep that list handy, like a menu, so when you're in burnout mode, it's easier to find and focus on what might help you feel better. They can be tasks that require variable levels of preparation, time commitment, and payoff so that you have a wide range of options. Ideally, every person would get some dedicated time each day to focus on resting and connecting, so your list can include lots of ideas that fit variable time frames. If you have a lot of time, you can choose more time-intensive activities and save the shorter ones for days when you have less time.

These coping skills need to be designed to support you in the moment *and* in the future. For example, maybe you like to unwind with a glass of wine, but you don't want to drink until you're drunk and hungover because you'll have a whole new set of challenges on your hands, and future you is gonna be pretty annoyed by this problem-compounding attempt to disconnect.

Don't overdo it on snacks, or exercise, or caffeine, or shopping, or even hot showers (we wanna look out for your water bill because nobody has time for some huge water bill). Rest activities in these categories have higher benefit ratios when there's moderation and balance between current you and future you. Generally, we don't want you to do anything that may cause later problems for the sake of current solutions.

In fact, the kinds of self-care we are describing here are rooted in kindness and compassion for yourself. The world is hard enough; start with kindness for yourself and watch that kindness spread. We have to stop these habits where we hurt ourselves when we feel miserable, which in turn piles on more misery. Kindness is revolutionary, unexpected, and exactly what you need and deserve.

## A Plan for Your Physical Self-Care

Bonnie has learned that she's way more likely to be on edge, too tense, or too snippy if she hasn't had enough water. There's something about that "I'm a little too thirsty/maybe dehydrated" feeling that makes her feel really close to the edge. For Faith, it's low blood sugar. Every irritating situation will push her anger button until her internal thermometer tells her it's time to explode. When really, if she would just have a little snack, her reaction would be to say, "Well, clean it up then" and move on.

Here's some feedback that Bonnie gives clients, and it almost always annoys them, so she's gonna annoy you with it too: You must literally do the things you need to do to feel like a human. Drink water. Eat food. Get sleep. Move your body. See your friends. There is a reason that many 12-step recovery systems tell you to watch for HALT. You are far more likely to relapse if you are hungry, angry, lonely, or tired.

Yes, you bought this book and the first piece of advice was "drink more water" and sorry not sorry because it's legit. You need basic care to feel your best. Sometimes, your best still feels crappy as hell, we know. And we know that more water and better nutrition won't fix things. But they do help, and they give you some power to do the things within your control to change your outlook.

Pause here and do a mental scan of your body.

- What is your body asking you for?

- Have you been moving as much as you'd like?

- Do you have areas of tension? What do those areas need to loosen?

- Have you done your annual wellness exams recently?

- Are you hydrating and eating food that fuels you?

- Are you sleeping okay? (Sorry, that's a loaded question for a lot of parents!)

- Are you spending time with people who care about you?

Based on your answers to these questions, you can begin to create an intentional plan to increase your capacity for self-care.

## A Plan for Your Mental/Emotional Self-Care

Did you know . . . Americans are not terribly good at leisure?

We are good at work. And many of us will work way too much, in our homes or in a workplace, because we feel a strong sense of identity in that sphere of our lives. We will work because we have to, obviously, to pay bills and eat food and stuff. But we also work because we live in a culture which values being busy. If we work a lot and are busy, we can use this excuse to avoid social things ("Oh, that sounds great, but I'm so busy!") or to avoid being at home ("Oh, I can't help with chores today, I'm so busy!") or to avoid feeling our own feelings or discomfort ("Oh, I don't want to feel sad today, I'm so busy!").

The trouble with busy is that it always reaches a breaking point. No one can stay busy enough for long enough for all the things we are avoiding to actually go away. By focusing on mental/emotional self-care, we can increase our capacity for dealing with the discomfort instead of avoiding it with work.

Take some time to discover (or rediscover) who you are in your spare time. Are you taking the time you need for yourself to feel like a whole person, not just parent, employee, business owner? What do you need to add to your life to make your self-care identity just as defined as your work identity?

Pause here and contemplate

- Who are you in your spare time? Who do you want to be?

- Are you engaging in a hobby you enjoy?

- Do you have time alone?

- How is your mood? How often do you feel stressed, down, or lonely? What about happy, content, or joyful?

- What are your memories of joy from childhood?

- When was the last time you had fun?

- Do you need more support than you are currently getting? (Could mean family/friends, therapy, or changes in work schedule.)

## Self-Care in Other Parts of Your Life

Self-care doesn't only apply to your body and your mind. Here are some other things you may need to attend to to make sure your cup is full:

- Assessing substance use

- Considering budget and finances

- Reviewing and adjusting daily routines

- Caring for your physical space (like decluttering or cleaning out a closet)

Now you've got a lot of new information about your needs and you're learning to listen to your body. The next step will be to spend more time in your mind.

# Speak Kindly to Yourself

In preparation for doing kind things for yourself, you need to assess your self-talk to make sure that's full of kindness too. There is a prominent attitude about "tough love" that we need to talk about here. The idea that we need to be harsh, or hard on ourselves or others, to see real changes in behavior is harmful. Real and lasting behavior change comes to people in relationships where they are loved enough to feel safe with mistakes. Where they can try things without fear of reprimand or shame. Where they feel encouraged to show creativity and problem solving and grit. Love and forgiveness make us feel like we can keep trying.

Tough love doesn't support any of that good stuff. It's driven by shame and perfectionism and burnout culture, and it's overwhelmingly ineffective. Tough love is toxicity masquerading as motivation, and we've all got to stop listening to it.

When you're working really hard, but still feeling like you're not doing enough, what you *do not* need is a load of tough-love bullshit. What you *do* need is help, and you have to ask for the help you need from the folks who love you. But you're much less likely to ask for that help if you don't believe yourself worthy of it. If you're supporting yourself with positive self-talk, you'll feel more like it's worth it to reach out and ask for the things you need to lighten your load.

We are asking you to grow your ability to have self-compassion[3], which is the practice of being gentle and kind

---

3 The work of Dr. Kristin Neff encapsulates all these benefits of self-compassion and more. You can find her at SelfCompassion.org.

with yourself in the face of feelings of inadequacy or failure. Self-compassion is nonjudgmental and isn't based in comparison to others. Self-compassion is built by being kind to yourself, practicing mindfulness, and considering our shared human experiences. Every single person will make at least one mistake; we will all face limitations and fall short of our expectations. Being mindful of these common aspects of humanity can take away the pressure we feel to be perfect or infallible. Criticism of our own perceived failures can result in shame, which in turn can make us timid so we can avoid further mistakes. Self-compassion makes room, though, for us to have a clearer perspective on those mistakes.

Spend some time over the next few days and take inventory of your self-talk. What do the observers in your head sound like? Ideally, those commentators have a reasonably realistic view of your effort and abilities. Additionally, they sound kind and supportive . . . while still holding you accountable. These voices are compassionate.

For most of us, though, the critics in our heads are not this way; they are a reflection of the messages we got growing up. If you listen closely to those voices, they probably aren't saying things you actually believe, they are parroting things they have heard others throw at you in anger or disappointment. And often, those voices are loud as hell, so they are hard to drown out.

Partly, the brain's tendency to hold that criticism in high regard is protective. We want to chastise ourselves so we can both avoid mistakes and control the level of chastisement, instead of having an outside observer chastise us.

Often, in session, therapists ask people to identify these voices/ideas and connect to the underlying fear. What are you trying to protect yourself from by using this hard self-talk?

The next step is realizing that the negative voice is loud as hell because it is afraid, and it doesn't feel hope, and it has to shout because it's panicked.

It's the loudest dude at your local school board meeting; he's there acting wild because he's scared and thinks no one will listen if he doesn't scream. But we can't let that guy make all the decisions for us. We can thank him for his input and continue to gather more information, but his voice can't be the only one in the chorus.

So that's the next step in this positive self-compassion journey. Can you identify that loud-ass Negative Nelly in your mind and find out what she's afraid of? Further, can you thank her for looking out for you? Can you reassure her that, even if no one is berating you, you've got the situation under control?

Over time and with practice, you'll be able to identify your self-talk and self-energy as separate from Scared at the School Board and Negative Nelly (or your parents, or an abuser, or a mean middle school girl, or a shaming church leader). Your authentic critical voice is probably gentle but firm. Your true protective energy is able to absorb derision from the other critics in your mind and synthesize it into meaningful feedback, which you can then decide to listen to or disregard.

Nobody has ever changed behavior because they were chastised into doing so; people change briefly, or get better at sneaking around, or give up completely, but it's not sustainable change. People can enact new behaviors if the relational energy supports it. Your job is to create a space for yourself where the energy supports you doing what you need, and that's a space rooted in kindness and accountability. So, if there's something you're saying to yourself that you wouldn't say out loud to your favorite person because it is absurdly mean or dismissive, don't say it to yourself. You approach others in your life with kindness, forgiveness, flexibility . . . you deserve those things too.

Interrupt any harsh or negative commentary from the Critical Chorus with a gentle "I'm doing my best" and a reminder that practice makes progress happen. You will slip back into Negative Nelly space pretty frequently at first because it's what you've been used to; it's a habit. You can change your habits, of course, by paying attention to the thoughts and the associated fears. But you're not going to do that 100 percent right away. In fact, you may never make it to 100 percent; old thoughts, especially those based in fear, can hold their default status for a long time (maybe forever, if the fear is strong enough). That's okay!

Over time, you'll recognize the default negativity, pause, assess reality, and move on from there. The default thought might be the first one that pops up, but it's not likely to be a true assessment of a situation or interaction. You're not going to do this observe-and-challenge protocol perfectly, but that's going to be okay, because you're creating a safe space to fuck up.

So when you do slip into negative self-talk (and you will!) recognize you have tools to experience the negativity and meet it with compassion. You can step in and avoid the spiral of self-disgust. You can support your behavior change and make it sustainable, which is more important than perfect anyway.

Difficulties come and go; meanwhile, your good qualities remain. Focus on those good qualities more often in an effort to stop beating yourself up emotionally.

# Commit to Your Self-Care Routines

Up to this point, we've been talking about plans for self-care. We've contemplated, we've listed, we've inventoried our needs, we've cultivated our self-compassion. Now what?

First, another reminder that you are valuable and worth taking care of. Your commitment to yourself needs to reflect that belief in your value as a human person who is worthy of care and compassion.

Now we can synthesize your lists into action plans. Reflecting on your physical, mental/emotional, and other needs, pick one or two things that feel doable within your current capacity and consider them through the lens of these questions:

- Do these ideas fit your budgets of time and finances?

- Will you have adequate support for these ideas?

- Do you need additional elements for these ideas (like a designated space in your house, or childcare at a specific time, or equipment)?

- How will you hope to feel if you make these ideas a reality in your routines?

- What is your current capacity in relation to your overall possible capacity? For example, maybe today feels like a 4/10. Will these ideas fit into a 1/10 day?

Bonnie often encourages clients to consider options for different-ability days. If you have a day with a bad chronic pain flare, or hit a depressy day, you're maybe not going to be able to do as much of your routine as you want. What's the minimum you need to do to get through a day feeling taken care of? What's the opposite end of that spectrum, when you feel 10/10 and can do everything you want? We aren't making self-care routines for how you felt yesterday or how you will feel tomorrow; what's your true capacity for today?

Further, your capacity includes many factors. It's how you feel physically, how well you slept, your stress levels, your health, your to-do list . . . and it's all the things your kids need too! An ideal balance of self-care for parents has to factor in all of the roles and obligations we possess. The argument we are making here, however, is that your self-care has to be included as an integral piece of your day and tasks.

To drop it in priority means that it will eventually slide off your radar altogether, and the feelings of burnout will slide in to replace it. Your needs exist in balance with the needs of your kids; yours don't disappear. Conversely, your kids don't stop needing you to show up because you've got mandatory self-care routines now. You can't neglect them, and you can't neglect yourself.

How do you find this balance for your family?

- List what you believe are your obligations to others in your life.

- Assess the list for anything you could drop or delegate.

- Consider your current available time. Is there any part of your schedule that you could rearrange to accommodate better balance?

- What does your ideal balance look like? How would you feel if you achieved it?

- What's your plan for days that aren't ideal?

- How will you include your self-care as a priority if there is an emergency or other conflict?

# Have Clear Boundaries

The idea that parents need to devote every available instant to our kids is not realistic and not fair to any of us, regardless of what our work/life/parenting demands look like.

Bonnie is a mom who works outside the home. For her to make that work, she requires clear boundaries between her roles, otherwise she tends towards burnout. She's committed to being super present at work when she's there, and she has a specific ritual to help her leave work at work. This way, when she's home, she can be all in on being a mom. And when her kid goes to bed, Bonnie can be present in being a good partner to her husband.

She uses these boundaries to keep mom-guilt at bay. She's only one person, and has a lot of roles to play, and she tries to minimize guilty feelings because they distract from that all-in-and-present approach. If she's at yoga class, she's *at* yoga class, present and focused, and she'll be a better mom, wife, therapist, and person because she did that.

There are a lot of ways to set clear boundaries between parenting and other parts of your life, so just as we did with self-care planning, let's talk about some ways to achieve this.

Consider:

- What are the roles you fill in your life and family?

- How do you feel about the current boundaries in those roles?

- Do you feel you need strict or clear-cut boundaries? Or is a general structure okay for you?

- How can you conceptualize these boundaries? Do you need phone reminders or a calendar or an accountability buddy?

- How will you review those boundaries regularly to make sure they are still working?

Once you've got some of this brainstorming done, you can better understand your boundaries and communicate them clearly to the folks who need to know about your needs.

# Manage Your Mental Health

Sometimes self-care goes beyond coping skills you can do on the fly. Even the ideal, most beautifully balanced self-care routine might not be enough to help you feel your best. If you're doing everything in your control, and you still feel shitty more days than you want to, it could be time to consider adding a professional to your plan.

Bonnie and Faith are both therapists who have therapists. We know the value of having a place to process, get support, and work on our triggers and coping skills. Bonnie takes antidepressants, which she had to start the year her daughter was born because, holy shit, postpartum anxiety is real and debilitating. To do her best to be a functional parent instead of a wobbly mass of anxiety-goo, the meds and therapy are important additions to her overall self-care plans. Faith has also been on antidepressants and still uses whole-food supplementation, herbs, bodywork, and even (*ugh!*) exercise, to stitch together a brain and body that functions with as few glitches as possible.

Consider the following questions:

- What's the status of your mental health currently?

- How does the way you feel emotionally or mentally affect you day-to-day?

- Do you feel you have the space and time you need to learn about yourself?

- Think about your own experiences growing up. How would you describe your mood as a kid?

- Did the adults in your life struggle with mental health? How would you have known if they did

Many clients in session with Bonnie reflect on those questions and find that their parents' mental health struggles did impact their lives, even if they may not have had the words at the time. Sometimes it felt like a general funk through the house. Or maybe it was in the form of a parent who had a hard time getting out of bed or staying off substances. But other times it is more understated; a mom who loses her temper in a flash, or a dad who is quietly seething at a dinner table. Sometimes it is a feeling of "Some feelings weren't okay and I didn't know why."

Our parents and their parents didn't necessarily have the same views of mental health care that Gen-X and millennial parents do. Those generations didn't have the access to therapy or meds that we have now, and there was a hardcore stigma to needing or wanting those things anyway. That stigma persists in many communities and it may even be something you feel yourself. What messages did you get from your parents or grandparents about experiences with mental health?

If you have a mental health issue that interferes with your overall functioning, you know that managing it, even on a good day, can be hard. You know that the exhaustion and stress of juggling all the parts of your own life can trigger mood changes, insomnia, substance use, or even suicidal ideation. We talk with clients all the time who are extremely worried about the effects of their own mental health on their children and the people they love. Your mental health, like all health issues, deserves to be met with compassion and a comprehensive treatment plan.

Be proactive about creating the treatment plan you need in order to address your symptoms as thoroughly as possible. Do you need talk therapy, meds, inpatient treatment, weekly support groups? Is the treatment plan you're on now meeting your needs or does it need adjusting? We are living in unprecedented times; adjust your treatment as often as you need to help you keep up. If you need a place to start, we recommend connecting with your primary care provider. That's a person who likely knows your medical history and can support you in finding community resources and referrals to mental health care.

# BUILD AND NURTURE YOUR TEAM

*F*amilies come in all shapes and sizes. Parenting can be incredibly isolating and can feel very lonely. Particularly when you're parenting younger kids who don't have the structure of a school day or social life to connect you to other parents. Your location, access to transportation, and even the season can factor into your ability to meet other parents. For families who have newborns in snowstorms and flu season, or families living in triple-digit summers, and everyone in between, there are a lot of factors that affect the ability to connect. But it's so important that you do! Sometimes it can feel like you've got to go it alone, but most of the time, you don't. Connect with other parents for support, relief, care, and friendship.

If you are raising kids as a single parent, you know all about the need to intentionally build a support system and a team for yourself and your kid. If your family structure is of the more traditional variety, maybe you are most in need of a reminder that this needs to be done, because you and a partner share the load. But it's still imperative for you to have outside connections. Forming authentic and supportive bonds with other safe and healthy adults who care about your kids is good for you and them.

But you do need to make sure the other adults in your kid's life are safe and healthy. Safe adults are people who respect your boundaries and those of your kid. They are thoughtful and helpful without bragging about it or hoping for something in return. They have good communication, and you think of them as reliable.

How do you recognize other adults who you feel good about? We hope you can trust your gut, but it's also worth learning to verify. Ask lots of questions when you meet someone new. Time is a good test to see if someone is consistent or if you notice some red flags. So give them plenty of your own time before you let them around your kids. Creeps can hide their creepiness for a while, but most people can't hide it for that long. If anything about another adult causes you to question their motives, it's okay to take some time away from that person to assess your response and gather more data. A quick online search is probably not the worst idea either.

Sometimes, people come into our lives and we don't notice any red flags. We've gone through the process and feel like it's a good fit. If your kid brings you any experiences that contradict that, please believe them and take a step back from the relationship while you assess the situation. The most important trusted adult in your kid's life is you.

# Find a Good Babysitter

A good babysitter is someone that does *exactly* what you say to do and doesn't give you any drama about your instructions. They are safe and reliable, come with good references, and understand that kids need and benefit from solid boundaries.

Hint: this person is usually someone you pay, not a family member. Family members are great for free childcare, sure, but they will 100 percent send your kid back to you as a sweaty, sugared-up, over-stimulated demon. This is not meant to be ugly about family members . . . it's just true. That's the role of grandparents, aunts, uncles, cousins: to give your kid the ice cream at 11:00 p.m., the let's-not-nap-right-now afternoons, the time to watch too much TV. That's great and kids need that free and fun space to explore with safe people. Bonnie remembers fondly the mornings she spent with her Granny watching *Perry Mason* reruns and eating handfuls of marshmallows straight from the bag; your kids will appreciate those types of memories too.

But please, occasionally pay a babysitter that follows your rules about naps, food, and everything else, and then go enjoy your child-free time with the knowledge that the demon living within your adorable child will stay at bay for now.

Finding balance between paid childcare and the free help your family or friends may offer is important for your feelings of community and support, and it's important for your kids to feel that as well. Also, if you have several options for help with childcare, you're more likely to find the flexibility to meet your own needs without relying too heavily on one free option or the paid option.

Where do you find this paid option, though? Start by asking in your network; who are other parents using for childcare? Maybe it's a neighborhood high school student who's done CPR training. Bonnie has often relied on people who watch her kid in other capacities, like the after-school care staff at preschool. They've been background checked, come with references, and already know the kids they care for. There are also websites that will background check people. And most larger cities have ways of looking up arrests and trials that were conducted within their jurisdiction.

Trust your parental instincts about who is a safe caregiver for your kids. Bonnie has a set of standard questions she asks her kid after time with a babysitter (paid or not). They include: What did you like about spending time with Ms. X today? Was there anything you didn't like? Did anything happen that you were asked/told to keep secret or not tell?

Once you've got a caregiver you trust, really nurture that relationship. This person is a key part of your support system and you've got to treat them that way. Give them plenty of lead time whenever possible to show you value their time and plans. Share their information with other parents to increase their income potential. Return home at the time you said you would, and be in communication about any delays. Pay them (in cash or trade or whatever your arrangement is) as if you are entrusting them with your most valuable possession. Treat them like a professional. Set clear expectations with your child so they aren't disrespectful while you're away. Solid childcare is so very valuable; you'll be very lucky to have such a person you can rely on.

# Bulk Up Your Support System

You don't have to do all this alone. If there are supportive fellow adults around you, ask for help. Not only do you not have to do it alone, you probably can't! There will be times you need something from your support system. That means you're going to have to (1) understand your need, (2) ask for the help, and (3) accept the help when it's offered. And those are three vulnerable emotional states many people will work quite hard to avoid.

How do you know you need help? And how will you get it?

- What emotions come up when you think about needing help?

- What do you need to feel more comfortable with asking for help?

- Who is on your list of reliable adults now?

- How can you contact these people?

- What would it be like for you to ask them for help?

- What kinds of help might you need? Financial, emotional, transportation, etc.?

- Are some people okay to ask for some kinds of help but not all kinds of help?

- How could you show appreciation for the people who show up for you?

The work of being in relationship with other humans is an investment. You invest in the people in your support network and they invest in you. Sometimes you have a lot of relational energy to invest in the group but other times you need to make withdrawals from the group. The reciprocity of relying on other folks is a key part of existing in relationships and communities.

Maybe these potential helpers aren't so obvious, or you still need to find them. Get creative!

Bonnie was pregnant and met a group of other moms online because they all liked the same podcast. Bonnie and those 172 other moms have formed a real and serious bond over the years; babies have been born, relationships have dissolved, jobs have been gained and lost . . . life has happened for them online, and they cheer for and mourn for and love each other. If one of them is too quiet, they reach out. They send flowers and cards to one another. They never miss a birthday. These people are among Bonnie's most valued friends even though the relationships are "virtual." That podcast has stopped production, but the group remains.

If you want to connect with other adults, you may have to briefly step out of your parent role. Yes, you're most likely looking for other parents, but that's probably not enough common ground to form a meaningful connection. You want to spend time with other parents who also share some of your values and interests. Look around you for options like that. Is there a group of moms hanging at the library? Dads at the donut shop? A social media group of people who are just as excited about macramé crafts as you are? A group of parents who spend weekends registering voters and sharing childcare responsibilities?

There are cool people out there, and they have kids too, so they recognize parts of your story as their own. You can connect with them and feel support.

It's not only other parents who can join your support team though. There are probably child-free folks in your life who have empathy and understanding for the complications kids add to hangouts and scheduling and who want to give you some support where they can. Or you can seek out child-free groups and spaces to make your parent role less central to the formation of new relationships and access a whole new sector of people to add to your support network.

# Parents Can Still Have Fun and Fulfilling Sex

For many adults, sex and physical intimacy are important ways to feel connected to other people and to our own selves and bodies. When we add kids to our lives, our available time and energy will shift to accommodate. Bonnie and Faith work with a lot of clients in this arena, because that shift can be incredibly complicated. For those of us who have sex, the ways we engage in these connections may change after the addition of kids into our lives.

Over the course of a lifetime, sex and sexuality change in myriad and thoroughly researched ways. For Bonnie and Faith, there have been some generalized patterns and struggles that show up in their sex therapy work with people who are parents. These generalizations are presented here to give you a chance to assess and understand your own journey. With a more clear understanding, we hope you'll be able to make any positive changes you want and that you'll feel empowered to communicate those feelings. Or, if no changes feel needed right now, you can communicate that too!

Parents of newborns tend to struggle with many physical factors that can affect sex and intimacy. Bodies that have given birth may have incisions and sutures that need time to heal and be cleared by a medical professional. Nursing, sleep interruptions, and loss of routines also affect the desire to connect physically. Emotionally, adding a newborn can be a real shock; parents can feel a wide range of huge emotions from overwhelmed, jealous, or scared, to joyful and euphoric.

Those kinds of variations can make connecting with partners really difficult. The guidance we give people in this stage of parenting is to make sure you are taking time to communicate. You may not connect sexually for a time period after having a newborn, and that's okay. It doesn't mean sex will never come back or that something is wrong in your relationship. But it does mean that parents need to be talking to one another openly and supportively about the feelings and needs they have for sex or physical connection.

Parents of toddlers and preschool kids often don't have the same physical limits as newborn parents but dang are these parents tired! Parents in this stage are on the move; they chase, and play, and manage meltdowns, and get sticky, and change diapers, and quietly cry through more than one episode of *Bluey* every day. They are exhausted and feel "touched out" because preschool kids are often very physical. This stage of parenting can be time and identity consuming, and that seems to be the main struggle for these parents. Bonnie and Faith work with these folks to reconnect to themselves as adults and partners by helping them carve out the time it takes to do that. These partners need dates and fun together so they can connect and recharge.

Parents of school-age kids are also tired, because school-age kids are busy as hell. They play sports and instruments, they go on field trips, and they get puberty mood swings. Elementary and middle school students are finding their identities and often that means *activities*. And activities for kids now are pretty different from when we were kids. Extracurriculars can require big investments of money and time and can be very disruptive to parents.

When Bonnie was a kid, her mom made her try every sport because joining the team was relatively cheap and kept Bonnie busy with something besides reading books and daydreaming about boys. And Bonnie was not, nor has she ever found an ability to be, a team sports kind of person. But it was okay to try a lot of stuff and be bad at it. That is not the experience Bonnie sees her own kid having. There's tremendous pressure to specialize early, and there's not as much space for exploring. That means that parents of school-age kids are often focusing on this aspect of life, and not on their own relationships, hobbies, or development.

These parents need a good network of other people so they can trade responsibilities. One family can do a weekend of drop-offs and pickups while you connect with a partner, and then you can return the favor next weekend. That kind of trade gives partners time to talk about anything that's not meal plans or schedules, and that's important for their feelings of connection.

Parents of older kids often show up opposite of school-age parents. Older kids are more independent and can manage more of their own responsibilities. This gives parents of older kids more time of their own, which, in theory, means their relationship can come back closer to center stage. That's the dream! But what we see with a lot of partners in this stage is that the strain of all the previous parenting iterations have left them feeling unsure.

Unsure of how to reconnect and understand a partner who is likely very different after the years of parenting. Unsure if they are even interested in their partner anymore, or if they are interested in trying to be interested. The chronic disconnection parents endure finally catches up to them at this stage. These parents need guidance in meeting each other with curiosity and tolerating uncertainty.

Whatever the parenting stage, there are a few common themes that can help with connection through sex or physical intimacy. Generally, it's helpful to have a space that is dedicated to adults where privacy is more available, like a room with a door that shuts and locks. It's helpful to have clear communication with partners about likes, dislikes, energy levels, and schedules.

Open dialogue helps partners feel respected and loved, and those are the feelings that are important to keeping connected even when physical intimacy isn't happening. Additionally, it can be helpful to reassess your definitions of sex and see if less patriarchal definitions fit your life better right now, like focusing on cuddling, foot rubs, and other "sensual but nonsexual" touching. Communicating these boundaries can help partners get what they need without feeling pressured.

We know that all sexual relationships are unique and different, and adding a kid to your family will affect those relationships in varying ways. We recognize that not all sexual partners will experience a dip in sexual activity and we are very excited for those people. We've also heard many people discussing their changes in sex life in therapy and want you to know that if you're having a hard time in this zone of your life, you're not alone. There are a lot of ways to be creative and supportive as you navigate this together.

# Practice (and Create) Cultural Traditions

Ethnic culture. Religious culture. Family culture. Having tradition creates security and meaning in everyday life. Human beings are really wired for ceremony. If the tradition is we go out for burritos on Friday nights, that may be just as sacred as a First Communion ceremony.

Discuss these traditions in practice. Talk about the why. Talk about the history of the practice. Let your kids see that it isn't random, but is steeped in real tradition. When Faith's kids were younger, Burrito Friday was the one day where they were all home early enough to go out to dinner and no one had to get up early the next morning. It's also nice after a long week to not have to cook or clean up, and we are all burrito fans.

But more than just getting a burrito with extra guac, she loved looking forward to time with her kids when she got to hear about their week and just hang out and chill without other shit going on. The family traditions you create in your own home are important to your family culture, are super fun, and can be very flexible. What are some of the ways your family has created these unique traditions?

Further, how do you participate in the wider cultural traditions of your heritage? What feels important from your own childhood that you'd like your kids to experience? How do you learn about your heritage and is there more you want to know? How do you feel your cultural experience influences your life or your space in the world?

Discussing and exploring cultural traditions in a wider sense is important to help kids have a broad understanding of the world and the ways we are interconnected. All people feel joy, and grief, and kinship. The ways we mark these experiences are beautiful and fascinating. How does your family welcome a baby? Is it different from the way your neighbors welcome a baby? What about grief and celebrations of life?

Sociologist Émile Durkheim wrote about this concept as "collective effervescence," humans coming together at a specific time and place to share thoughts and actions. Belonging to something beautiful and important and participating in cultural experiences is a wonderful part of being a human. What collective effervescence does your family celebrate?

# Choose a Family Motto, Guide Word, or Value

Your family is a team. Your team is unique. There is no other family like your family. Isn't that fantastic? That's something to celebrate and make a big deal of. That's something that deserves a souvenir T-shirt! But what will you put on your T-shirt? May we suggest an outrageous family motto?

Sit together with your family and brainstorm some words or values that you appreciate or that have meaning to you as a group. Come to a consensus on a few words that can guide your family life and decisions out in the world. Bonnie's family value is "kindness" and her family chose it together. They can revisit it when they feel lost, confused, or angry. Bonnie can say to her daughter, "Our family values kindness. Does this action fit our value?" or, "Remember: we agreed to choose kindness." It's a gentle reminder that they have a family goal of doing no harm to each other or others in their lives.

Faith's family rule was taken from Wil Wheaton. As mentioned in her book *Unfuck Your Adulting*, "Don't be a dick." It was a funny reminder to do the best you can. Not that you will never make mistakes, but that you are always trying to be considerate (and kind!) in the process of your daily life.

It's great if your motto is easy to remember, maybe a little fun, and acceptable to shout in public as you drop your kids off at school. Some additional Scott family faves include, "Don't talk about it, be about it!" and, "Be a problem solver, not a problem maker!" Because they are that kind of obnoxious family. Your family mottos are yours and can be as obnoxious and/or meaningful as you want.

How does your family talk about values?

- What are the values that bring you together as a family?

- What ideals guide your decisions and activities?

- How do you keep those principles at the forefront of your mind?

- Will they fit on your souvenir T-shirt?

# Be on the Same Team with Other Adults

Ideally, you and anyone else you're managing a household with are going to be on the same page about some of the basics: values, house rules, how you want to handle discipline, what bedtime is. That can mean a lot of communicating and disagreeing while working toward that common messaging. Additionally, you want to really look like a team and you don't want your kids to see one parent taking a lot of responsibilities while the other coasts through life without spending that kind of energy. Raising kids can feel more manageable if you've got good communication between adults.

Bonnie and her husband have a once-a-month CEO meeting where they meet on the couch after their kid is asleep, with actual pens and paper calendars, and review what needs to get done around the house, fun things they want to do, work commitments, school/kid commitments, and time for a date night. The agreement is that they can make minor changes to the schedule created during the CEO meeting through a text or a quick "oh hey, this changed" conversation, but if it's a significant change, they meet again and make sure they are on the same page (they are so fun at parties . . . but also they actually make it to your parties because that invitation was discussed at the CEO meeting).

Aim for as equal distribution as possible in things like chores, bedtime routines, cooking and cleanup, and all the other necessary tasks you need to complete to keep a house running. If you're partnered, have real conversations about this with your partner, and find a balance that avoids relying on stereotypes or burdens one partner over another. Bonnie knows a couple that spent a whole week writing down the minutes they spent doing chores and then reviewed at the end of the week and redistributed tasks in areas that weren't balanced and fair. Maybe you're not data-driven to that level; that's cool. But take time to examine your processes and commit to balance and an equal distribution of labor.

And discuss with your children that the tasks are divided in a way that makes the most sense for your family. Maybe one adult stays home, so they do more of the work around the house. Maybe Mom cooks because she *likes* cooking, not because that's what women do. Talk about how those roles are decided and why, rather than presume they understand. Otherwise, the gender norms in media will raise a false flag for them.

Spend some time talking with your kids about all the ways a family can look and function. Emphasize the ways in which everyone in your family works together for the health and happiness of the group. List the ways that you care for and about each other, and think of ways you can show appreciation for that. Talk about different family structures that your family or their friends' families could take on: hetero parents, same-sex parents, single parents, grandparents-as-parents, stay-at-home parents, adoptive/foster parents, and the ways we can create families out of our friends.

Think of the language that you want to model, and negotiate it as needed. Faith uses the term "bonus children" to include both bio and bonus kiddos—a term she borrowed from Jada Pinkett Smith. She may also use the term "nonbio niblings" to describe the kids in her life that she considers family because "stepchildren" and other terms felt icky. She will cheerfully say she has thirteen kids. When people look askance, she responds with "I only actually gave birth to a couple of them . . . but they're all mine!" She also respects how her kids relate to each other ("That's my brother" or "That's my cousin"), because it's about the emotional content of the relationship, not the biological family tree structure.

If you have more than one parent/adult care provider in the household, each adult needs time each week to be alone in the house, time with other grownups without kids around, and everyone-is-together family time. That might be a lot to juggle, hence the need for schedule synchronicity. It's doable with good planning and communication.

If you're having trouble agreeing, or learn that you're contradicting each other to your kids, please have that conversation sooner instead of later. Before the problems created bite everyone in the ass. If you are parenting with someone who absolutely refuses to follow the same rules that you have established, you have to assess if that relationship is sustainable. If your current partner is actively undermining you, you could probably really benefit from some therapy or coaching around your different parenting styles and how to better approach your kids as a team.

# Keep Your Cool with Your Co-Parent

If the person you're trying to co-parent with is not your current partner, that can add a lot of variables.

Approach your co-parent assuming best intent. Yes, even if they are your asshole ex who may not be operating with the best intent. We are going to start by presuming they are until proven otherwise. Because nothing will change if you constantly have your fight face on. Communicate calmly and stick to the facts, as in "I know you really wanted to bring the kids out this evening, but Jojo has a huge project due that I only learned about two days ago.[4] I bought the posterboard and printed out the images they need, but they still need to get it all together this evening before they do anything else because their presentation is in the morning, and this is the class they've been struggling in."

Hopefully, over time, even the asshole ex will come around and will want to communicate with you in the best interest of your kids. But if not, you may have to just own it and plan for it.

As in, "Mama and I have different rules about getting homework done. This means you'll have to learn and follow different rules in both households. I know that makes things confusing, but 'Mama doesn't make me do homework before TV!' won't change the rules in my house. This makes more work for you now, and I'm sorry about that, but it will make your life easier later when you need to adapt to different rules in different situations. Most people struggle with that, but you'll have good strategies because I'm going to help you learn to navigate these differences."

---

4 This is demonstrating that you aren't just dumping something on them, so hopefully they will embrace best intent in return.

Sometimes people can negotiate and agree together about things like custody, finances, and rules and can do so relatively smoothly. Oftentimes, though, emotions run high, and these agreements have to be made in court or with a mediator.

Which is all to say, this can be really difficult and really painful. Even when your ex is weaponizing every fucking thing, and you are feeling painfully wounded and in your feels, it benefits your kids to focus on your end goals.

The best advice we can give is to do the right thing even when no one else is. It's not fair that you have to be adult enough for both you and your ex, but time bears all of that out in the end. It takes a while and it's a painful process, but it keeps your kiddos from having to choose sides in the present and gives them a level of stability to look back on. Some of the things that help:

- Don't bad-mouth your ex. Even if they are trash and not in the fun Oscar-the-Grouch sense of the word. Let their relationship with your kids stand on its own, not be influenced by the relationship between the two of you. Either they will be better to their kids (thank fuck) or they will demonstrate quite handily how trash they are. Either way, your kiddos' relationship with your ex should be their relationship, not yours.

- Don't get triangulated into stuff. If your kiddo bad-mouths them or complains, turn that back toward their relationship with that parent whenever possible. Start with "Did you tell them you were uncomfortable with meeting the person they are dating? That sounds like a conversation the two of you should have." Obviously this doesn't apply to immediately dangerous situations like if they were driven by your ex who was raging drunk behind the wheel, but it absolutely applies to the tattley stuff kids do during a divorce to get a rise out of us. It doesn't mean accepting falsehood, however. If it is something along the lines of "Mom said you are a [fill in the blank with pejorative of your choice]," a conversation-ending response would be "That's not a true statement."

- Keep the issues between you and your ex between you and your ex. Don't parentify your kids, don't make them the person you talk to about this shit. Go get 73 therapies if you need to, but don't make it your kids' job. The message your kids hear should be some variation of "That's stuff between us and it's hard right now. But we are both your parents, we both love you so so so much, and we still a family even if we are no longer together. We are having to figure out how to do that well, and it's been hard, and it's taking more time than we want it to, thanks for being patient."

- (Try to) make preemptive rules with your ex about how certain things will be handled by both of you should they arise in the future. You can't plan for every contingency, and you can't make them act right, but you can act right and hope they will do the same. For example, you may think you are never going to date anyone ever again. And you may be right. But you may also change your mind. So a rule about how long someone new has to be in either of y'all's lives before they meet the kids is super important. And maybe even rules around how long before y'all tell each other, whether you want to meet new partners before the kids do, etc. If you are doing 73 therapies right now, this is a good thing to strategize with your therapist about, since they know the specifics of your situation.

- When all else fails, use the general rule that all of Faith's clients hear at some point. And that is to do the best you can with the information you have right now. Or, to put it in her tough-coach voice, "Ten years from now, will you be embarrassed about what you're doing right now?" She doesn't want you to ever be upset at yourself for doing the best you can in any situation, but especially in an acrimonious breakup, we feel very wounded and can behave in very wounding ways. So no matter how your ex is showing their ass, don't show yours. If you know better right now, and you know after the emotions have settled you'll recognize your behavior as shitty, don't do it. Future self will really be grateful to not need 73 more therapies to resolve that guilt.

# Navigating Different Values with Other Parental Figures

Some of the people on your family team are likely to not be totally on board with all your ideas, especially if you were drawn to the feminist, antiracist aspects of this book. Maybe it's the grandparents, your ex, the nuns at the school, or other people who have influence with your kids and that your kids likely look up to.

Later chapters in this book are filled with tools for talking with your kids about contentious issues, from prejudice they may experience or see in school to police violence, religion, and party politics. But how do you have those conversations with the other adults in your kid's life—or do you?

What boundaries do you feel you need in those relationships? For example, maybe it's okay for your mom to talk with you about politics, but you don't want her to talk about it in front of your kids. We determine our boundaries by paying close attention to our gut reactions and our responses to the ways we interact with people.

- Who are the people in your life that give you a strong negative gut reaction?

- What ideas do they have that you struggle with or do not want your kids to engage with at this time?

- Why is setting this boundary important to you?

- How will you communicate these boundaries?

- How will you enforce these boundaries?

- How will you respond when your boundaries are ignored or purposefully violated?

Furthermore, this may not be a discussion you're just having with adults. You may need to communicate these boundaries to your kids as well so they know your expectations. Boundaries are set to help keep everyone feeling safe.

- How do you want to discuss these boundaries with your kid?

- Do you want them to know if you have chosen to have a boundary discussion with an adult?

- How might the boundaries affect your kid's relationship with the adult in question?

- Do you want input from your kid about the boundaries you might put in place?

These boundaries likely look different in each relationship in your life. And that's complicated, yes, but that's the work. You want to explore progressive ideas and you're trying to unfuck your parenting. You also want to create a safe space for your kids to explore what these ideas mean for them. So you have to identify the relationships where that's safe and productive and where it's not. Any adults that would use name-calling, boundary violation, coercion, or anger in these types of conversations need to know from the start that those behaviors aren't accepted in interactions with your kids. If that means these topics are off the agenda completely, then that's what it means. Your boundaries need to be communicated from the beginning and need to be enforced consistently.

Sometimes when we start to think about boundaries, we imagine them like an electric fence. We think we need to be so rigid in the setting and communicating that we might as well make a royal proclamation. In practice though, our boundaries can likely be communicated in a much less dramatic way. It might be as simple as a text message when you're on the way to a family dinner, "Please remember that we do not want to talk about politics at this family dinner. We are gathering to celebrate our dog's graduation from obedience school and we won't let the spotlight stray from her accomplishments." Hopefully, the adults you're setting boundaries around will respond to some strategically placed orange traffic cones and you won't need any electric fences.

But you may need to have some serious and uncomfortable conversations with these adults, and this may result in some electric fence–style interventions if folks aren't willing to honor your requests. Even if you're thoughtful about creating reasonable guidelines, there may be significant resistance. Any shame you may have wrestled as you worked through this process yourself will be fresh and strong in people who haven't been on your journey, and shame often results in denial and defensiveness. Only you can do the risk/benefit analysis of setting these boundaries and maintaining these relationships. Your end goal is to keep your kids in a place that's emotionally safe for them to continue to explore what progressive ideas mean for them without feeling like they are a disappointment to any of the adults they admire.

# Navigating "Parenting" Kids That Aren't Yours

Whether it's your kid's best friend, your friend's kid, or your kid's teammates or classmates, you're going to run into other kids who look up to you. How do you navigate upholding your values (especially if *your* kid is right there) without alienating their parents? There are a couple different scenarios here.

One is your "bonus kids"—the kiddos you have a parental-type relationship with (cuz whoever their bio and/or legal parents are, they agreed to you being in their lives, or, the kids don't have any viable parent-people). Upholding your values is likely a bit easier in this scenario because you've been invited to be part of this kid's life; if the parent is in the picture, they probably know where you stand and share some of those beliefs.

Then, there are just "other people's kids." The kids who come into your life because your kid has chosen to spend time with them and who are now spending the weekend at your home and keep harassing the dog and are in desperate need of correction. Now, Faith grew up in the '70s and '80s on military bases. If you were at someone else's house and acted a fool, their momma would spank your butt and send you home. And as you walked in the door to your house, *your* momma would be hanging up the phone with an "I see, thanks for telling me, we'll take care of it." And then you got your butt spanked again. At least by your momma, and maybe a third time when your daddy got home. And because Faith was a sassy-mouthed little urchin, this probably explains why her butt is so flat to this day.

Normalized spanking doesn't happen anymore, which is clearly for the better. But it does mean that we gotta have the convo about our rules and other parents' rules and work with other families more proactively than reactively. And honestly, whether they are an all-in bonus kiddo or a member of the neighborhood pack raiding your popsicle stash, being in contact with the parent-people who hold the actual legal standing in their lives is really important.

If it is a kiddo new to your abode, ask the dropping-off parent-person straight out, "Hey your kiddo is probably way better behaved than my weirdo, but if there is anything I need to bring up to them cuz our house rules may be a little different, how do they best hear stuff? Is there anything I need to be aware of that they struggle with? Anything in particular you need to hear back about or anything you want to handle yourself?" The best part of all this is that all kiddos will then know that all adults are a united front on expectations and they can't get sneaky.

For a full-on bonus kiddo, your role may get more fluid with their parents-of-record, but communication is still important. Even if it's a brief convo, more of an FYI, "This came up today, and it's totally already been addressed by . . ."

If there is a longer-term behavior or personality challenge at play with someone else's kid, then we need to set some serious boundaries. We can't set boundaries for other people, only for ourselves. One particular friend of Faith's older child wasn't invited into Faith's home (Faith's boundary) so Faith wouldn't have a smackdown with them over their expressed values and political symbolism and other stuff that was not her place to get into. Faith explained to Kid One that she wants everyone to feel safe in her home, and their friend's behavior would challenge that safety for other people, which made it not acceptable. Faith didn't tell her kiddo not to be friends with this person, but she did control how this person could impact others who may be in Faith's home.

# CREATE A
# SAFE HOME

*I* f we're going to be good community members, it's helpful for us to purposefully cultivate a few skills that encourage growth of community. These are connection, kindness, and compassion. Connection starts at home, and kindness and compassion start with internal work—something it's never too late to learn, but it's a lot easier to learn as a kid than as an adult. Maybe you and your kids can learn together.

When Faith (Gen-X af) and Bonnie (Xennial who fits in nowhere) were growing up, all the world asked for or expected of our parental units was that they generally kept us alive. Most parents didn't take on the task of paying attention to the emotional needs of their kids back then. Everyone was expected to just toughen up. And those same parents (now grandparents) often grumble that these kids today are coddled and bratty instead of seeing the possibility that these young people are growing up in unprecedented times while navigating the inheritance of everything all the previous generations got wrong. They deserve a fighting chance, and having a nurturing home environment is the very best tool for doing so. Caring is not coddling, all right?

So this chapter contains our list of the internal, emotional shit kids need to have a fighting chance at success when they fly the nest. These are some ideas for how you can begin to incorporate a kid and their needs into your established adult life (while facing the fact that you may not feel like the adult in the room yet).

These are some approaches and topics you can use to open conversations about how you want your family to be and the ways you want your kids to be in the world. The ideas can be summed up as: "Be kind, be compassionate, be responsible, be supportive," because your goal is to create a space where your kids feel included and understood. We hope it's a guide that serves you in searching yourself and your family for the places you can be more empathic and more accepting of imperfections.

We also hope that you'll honor the gift you've been given by regularly reminding yourself (out loud, with a note on your mirror, with a pop-up calendar reminder) that even when parenting is hard af, it's an honor bestowed on us by the universe. That we have been paired with these people, to guide and love them, is no accident, and this deserves respect. We have to remember that we can hold conflicting ideas without our heads popping off our necks . . . we will enjoy our kids *and* be the people responsible for setting them straight in the world.

Fun fact. Two out of two authors of this book recognize that this section is a lot, in and of itself. And freely admit they are works-in-progress in this area. Zero percent of this book is designed to make you feel like a parenting failure, because you aren't. Also, we already have social media to do that. It is about the journeys that all of us are on so we can remember our prime directive (nerd joke!) as humans responsible for the care and feeding of other humans.

Take a few minutes to think about the following:

- What kind of parent do you want to be?

- What about your own upbringing do you want to pass down to the next generation?

- What about your own upbringing do you want to resolve and not pass down?

- How do you want to feel in your home? How do you want your kids to feel?

- How do you treat yourself when you make a mistake? How do you want to be treated?

- How do you treat your kids or family members when they make a mistake? How would you like to treat them?

# Create a Safe Home for Feelings of All Kinds

Any emotional baggage we don't deal with ourselves, we risk passing down to our kids.

Of course, we're talking about trauma here, and this wouldn't be an Unfuck book without getting right into it. Trauma is what you experience when something happens, big or small, that your nervous system can't cope with. If you can't soothe your system within a short period of time (roughly 90 days), your brain will create a reflexive association of danger with either the thing that hurt or scared you or a seemingly random detail your brain noticed in the moment. That's a trigger.

Even if you're not familiar with the concept of trauma, you've likely heard the word "trigger," and maybe not in a very kind or accurate light. Clinically speaking, a trigger is the stimulus that causes a trauma response. It could be anything, including an event, memory, or sensation, that results in an intense emotional response, regardless of your mood. That response will be involuntary and intense and can feel crippling. So maybe now you're afraid of ladders, but you could also panic when you smell cinnamon, or shut down completely when you hear yelling. It could be an uncomfortable quirk of your experience, or it could be full-blown post-traumatic stress disorder (PTSD) that prevents you from doing the stuff you need to do in life.

As language tends to do, the word trigger has morphed in popular culture from the classic definition of a PTSD-level reaction to mean anything that makes you feel uncomfortable. To understand your own experience of being triggered, you need to (1) notice your intense emotional reactions, and (2) be able to pay attention to what aspects of your life or interactions bring about intense emotional reactions. Are you having a response to a traumatic memory or reliving a traumatic moment? Are you feeling envious, angry, or shameful? Does the response look like fear, anger, shallow breathing, crying, tearfulness, or avoidance?

Our instinct is to avoid all of the situations or interactions that may emotionally trigger us, because it feels gross to be triggered and worked up. Especially when we're busy parents hanging on by a thread, and your stress levels and burnout may make you even more likely to experience triggers. But avoidance isn't a sustainable strategy. The more we avoid, the more activated we become.

Now we are on the lookout for anything that could be a trigger, and we are putting energy into predicting and avoiding those situations, and we are doing that on top of all the other emotional and physical labor we are asked to perform as parents and adults. Our brains and bodies can't maintain those levels of activation; it's exhausting. That's not to say that the work of healing isn't also exhausting, because it often is. But that's at least energy you're investing with a greater possibility of positive return.

And for parents, the chances of fallout from avoidant behaviors are especially high. The kids you are raising are watching you from the time they are born to gather cues about what is safe and what isn't. If you're feeling unsafe, or triggered, or avoidant of perceived or possible threats, your nervous system is sending signals to kids that they also need to be on high alert. It's easy to see how that cycle continues across generations, because we haven't always had the knowledge and tools we have now to talk about and heal our trauma. In working with your triggers and creating coping skills and healing, you're sending a really different message to your kids: bad things can and do happen, and we can learn the skills needed to heal without being avoidant.

There are long-term impacts of avoidance, one of which is the creation of a home where some feelings are okay but others are not. Your kids will learn about your avoidance, and most kids will work hard to avoid whatever makes you upset. Those kids are doing the emotional labor of adults, which is pretty unfair to them, and kids who never experienced what traumatized us may end up with our same triggers without really understanding why. Additionally, they may never learn the coping skills to deal with the shit life throws at them, either.

We've had so many clients who talk about how when they were growing up, there was no acceptable way to be mad, or sad, or maybe even too happy, depending on the triggers of the parents. If we as parents aren't aware of our triggers, depression, and anxiety (you know, all that baggage shit from our own lives), we may be subconsciously sending the message to our kids that some feelings aren't okay. When our kids inevitably feel those "not okay" feelings, and then we adults are triggered and losing our shit on them, we are teaching them they gotta stuff that emotion way, way down, because home isn't a place for that particular feeling.

Set out to make your home a place that's safe for feelings of all kinds. The big ones, the confusing ones, the hurtful ones. Home is where we can explore those feelings in a safe space. And that starts with you learning coping skills so that you can feel these feelings yourself. If you start noticing behaviors or responses that seem disproportionate to the stimulus, you may find that you're triggered by things in your home to the point of feeling out of control. For example, maybe you screamed and cried when your kid spilled jelly on the counter, or you snapped at everyone in the car for being too loud, or you zoned out every time your kid brought up a specific topic. If you feel like your response to triggers feels unsafe for you or others, therapy could be a really good investment for you. If that's not an option, you can start by practicing coping skills like the grounding exercise at the beginning of this book.

We know, yet one more thing that we are responsible for doing in order to not ruin our kids. But creating emotional safety is the big one, and it makes life way easier for everyone in the house, especially the parent-people. Talking about feelings is the best way to be proactive about addressing the more manageable mental health issues in hopes they will not become huge, untenable ones.

Start with small, doable convos, setting the standard that these are not elephant-in-the-room, closed topics of conversation. For instance, you might notice your kid is feeling sad and ask them about it, or check in with your friends about each other's feelings within earshot of your kids, or say "I was really excited!" when you're telling a story about what happened in your day. Then, when life gets really spiky, it will be easier to speak truth to pain because your family can all speak the language of emotion with less freaking out. These emotional conversations, big or small, can be handled as matter-of-factly as "the trash needs to go out to the curb" or "wash your hands, dinner will be on the table in three minutes."

There are no limits on feelings, but the actions used to show them need boundaries. Those boundaries will be different in every home and may require some conversations or workshopping to make sure everyone is feeling safe. For some of us who are healing from trauma, things like loud voices or slamming doors may be very frightening. For others, a frosty silence may be the most frightening sound of all. It's important to talk about how each person in your home responds to emotional cues so that everyone can regulate their responses for a more peaceful home.

In Bonnie's home, it's okay to feel angry, but it's not okay to slam doors. It is okay to say "Ugh, I need a minute!" and then go spend a few minutes in a bedroom or bathroom. When someone in your home is triggered, which happens even in the most thoughtful homes, it can be helpful to have a "take a break" agreement. The average person needs about twenty to thirty minutes to regroup after the flooding feeling of anger or fear. That twenty minutes is the time to tap into coping skills, self-care, reflection, and other return-to-safety processes. It is not the time to plan a loud and forceful argument about why everyone else in this exchange sucks. It's a time to take care of yourself so you can return to the discussion, event, or interaction in a way that's regulated and peaceful, setting everyone up for success.

## Exercise: Working with Your Emotions

Examine some of your own feelings and the ways you might recognize them in yourself. Look also at how you show them to others.

Ask yourself "When I feel happy, how do I know I feel happy? How do I show my happiness to people around me?" and continue going through emotions until you've got a solid list. It could look like:

- Happy: I know I'm happy when I feel lightness in my chest or a smile on my face. I like to show my happiness to others by smiling, telling them with words, or throwing confetti.

- Sad: I know I'm sad when my body feels heavy or I feel the pressure of tears behind my eyes. I don't like other people to see my sadness so I am not sure how I want to show that feeling.

- Hangry: I know I'm hangry when everything inconvenient feels like a huge hurdle. I want to recognize hangry for myself and take care of myself instead of showing that irritation to my family.

It may be helpful to use a tool like an emotion wheel. It's a visual representation that gives you a lot of words for emotions, and that increased vocabulary can be really useful if you're new to exploring emotions.

Once you've got your own list, then you can ask the other people in your home to make lists for themselves. You can include kids of all ages, and you can be creative in that process. You know your kids. Maybe they are glad to make a list. Maybe smaller kids need to draw or use modeling clay. Maybe teens need to make a playlist. The process is really just to show that you're a family that's open to talking about feelings.

Plan a time to sit and talk about your lists a little bit as a group. Learn more about the inner world of the people with whom you share your life and space. Decide together how you want to communicate feelings and decide what's okay and what's not.

# Listen to Understand Instead of to Respond

Take a moment and think about what it was like to have a conversation with your parents when you were younger.

- Whether the conversation was light or heavy in topic or tone, did you feel heard and welcomed?

- Were your opinions solicited?

- Were the emotional undertones seen and acknowledged?

- Or did you grow up in a family where "Kids are seen and not heard," or "You don't know; you're just a kid" were the basic beliefs? Or maybe whatever point you made was rebutted swiftly and unceremoniously?

- Were you allowed space to vent and think out loud, or were the adults in your life quick to try to rescue or problem solve?

- What parts of your childhood communication lessons do you want to carry on and what do you want to leave behind?

- What conversations can you remember where you felt valued and affirmed? What about shamed or misunderstood?

We all model the communication we grew up with, to some extent. There are parts of that that work and parts that don't, but to be able to actually, truly listen to another person is powerful. For your kid to feel they are understood by you creates a strong attachment and a safe space for all kinds of conversations, particularly the ones we are discussing in this book.

We don't get anywhere in any conversation if we are waiting for the chance to land a verbal KO. This world needs more (attempts at) understanding and less talking like we are in an online comments section. Tough topics don't need a "devil's advocate" or other adversarial approaches like mockery or condescension. (Even though a well-placed joke is a strong way to defuse tension, jokes can also derail a conversation and be used as a way to avoid a topic altogether; use humor sparingly.)

Listening is an art, which requires empathy and creativity, both being solid life skills for our little Padawans to learn. Truly listening to another person means you can identify (1) the content of what is being said, (2) some of the processing the person went through to choose the words they used, and (3) the emotional meaning behind what is being said.

There is a cheesy-but-reliable therapist trick for teaching empathic listening. When two people are in conversation, one person holds a physical object like a pillow or a TV remote or whatever is handy. The person holding the object gets to talk while the other listens. Then, the "listener" offers their understanding of what was said by the "speaker." When the speaker feels heard and understood, they can pass the object to the listener and the roles switch. If the "speaker" doesn't feel understood, they can continue holding the object and they can restate their position or rephrase for better understanding. Then the "listener" can try again. This is not a time for the "listener" to offer rebuttals, explanations, or defenses; it's a time to listen for content and feelings.

Typically, it takes about three rounds to get to the guts of the conversation, which is where you find the feelings, implicit bias, and beliefs. It's really interesting to do this exercise with people in your life, and your kid will like it because they will have all of your attention.

For example:

**Parent:** It's time to put on your clothes for school!

**Kid:** I hate those clothes! I won't do it!

**Parent:** That's a strong feeling. Can you tell me more about that? What's going on?

**Kid:** Nothing, but I'm not putting on any clothes. I'm not going to school today.

**Parent:** Help me understand; you usually love school. Are you maybe feeling a little nervous about your recital this afternoon?

**Kid:** Ugh, yes. And I am not ready to get dressed and go to school because then the recital will be there.

Really listening to another person gives us a chance to offer support and build deeper relationships and understandings with others. This also means we need to put aside our need to be right all the time because, actually, no one likes a know-it-all. Which is bad for Bonnie and her kid because they think almost every situation needs a "Well, actually . . ." But actually, people don't want your advice (even people who are asking for it, which is confusing, we know, but whatever). People want to feel heard and supported, actually, and being able to be that person for someone is a valuable human experience.

Instead of "Well, actually . . ." try some phrases like "That's interesting" or "What makes you think this?" or "How can I support you?" or "Tell me more about that" and then actually listen when your kid answers.

# Practice Patience

Faith will let you know how to do this if she ever figures it out. Heh.

But seriously, we live in such a rage-quit society, it's no wonder that it's so difficult to find people who are built to put in the time and effort to complete a long-term project. We carry tiny computers (that we sometimes use to make phone calls) with us at all times and have infinite human understanding available with the taps of a few buttons; it can seem like speed is the desirable thing. But so much of what is really worthwhile should take time. Finishing school or job training. Making an authentic risotto. Falling truly in love. Raising kids.

Give your kids lessons of patience where they are able to see the payoff at the end. Faith did this back in the day when her kids wanted a Wii. They made it a household savings task where all extra change everyone had went into a jar until the money was raised.

It took a while, and her kids would inspect the jar hopefully. But they also liked the game of filling the jar, even picking up pennies in the parking lot to add. Y'all change-droppers funded their Wii, just saying. This is what teaches them the value of perseverance.

And if you suck at being patient? Y'all, we feel you. And we feel it's important to own that in our out-loud voices with our kids as something we are all working on. As in, "I hate waiting, too! Let's figure out ways to be more patient together!" Or measure progress together or even just grumble about how much it sucks together. It can be good for us *and* be really difficult to do at the same time.

For Bonnie, conversations with her daughter around patience typically focus on the idea that everyone is doing the best they can with what they've got. There's a long line at the drive-through? Be patient because everyone's working hard. There's empathy in patience, and kindness too, and those are two key values for Bonnie and her daughter.

That's all well and good when they are waiting for burgers or whatever, but Bonnie does seriously struggle to maintain any sense of composure when her kid is the one taking forever. How can you maintain patience with your kid when you've asked them fifty bazillion times to put on their shoes or feed the pets or take out the compost? Bonnie has tried a lot of strategies for this, and she's not sure she's found one that really works long-term.

She has tried yelling (that's like, negative patience points so probably not that), cajoling (moves quickly to yelling, so probably not that), and even bribery (gets expensive quickly, so probably not that either). The thing that's worked the best so far is to give frequent reminders, like "We leave for school in twenty minutes and you need to be ready to go!" along with letting her kid deal with the natural consequences of her actions. If she doesn't do something on time, she's late to school (which she haaaaaates), or she's late to the birthday party and misses some of the fun, or she doesn't get to go with dad to the grocery store.

That way, Bonnie can do less patience-losing and have more conversations about decisions and their outcomes. Bonnie decided a long time ago that she doesn't like who she is when she yells and loses her temper, so she's done a lot of work around managing her activation levels with breaks or grounding techniques. And this is a reminder that parenting is often about making things work better most of the time. And the rest of the time, we're trying to keep little people alive long enough for their prefrontal cortex to kick in so they can manage their own lives.

It's not your kids' job to be parentable. It is your job to parent them anyway. How can you change your approach to be a more patient parent to them? What can you do for yourself that helps you lose it less often?

# Calm Your Tits

We all know how we are *supposed* to be. And when we hit the point where we aren't operating from that place, we try to force our way through. Sometimes we *can't*. Not in the moment. At some point, we need a break. And our kids need a break from our reactivity. You need to be aware of what sets you off and how to recognize when you are getting set off so you can step away and regroup. If you can assign a pinch hitter, do so. Faith and her dear friends who helped her co-parent literally call each other or tap each other on the shoulder and say, "Tag, you're it," and the relief parent comes up to bat.

If you're by yourself, that's okay too. Take a break and come back to the situation. For example, yes, we know we are supposed to comfort a crying baby, but if you are so activated by several hours of nonstop inconsolable colic, put the baby in a safe place and go take a shower. Run the vacuum cleaner to drown out the crying noise. The tenseness is breeding more tension, and there is no consoling going on. Faith had zero problem doing that when her kiddos were teeny. When they were embiggened, she would say "I need for us to both go to our rooms and calm down a bit so we can come back to this in a better way."

Calm-down time is great to incorporate with other consequences or behavior plans. For example, Bonnie's daughter has always had a list of consequences for when she makes decisions that are not in-line with those expected of her. The list was created when she was three, and has been adjusted slightly over time. It starts with the loss of a privilege and is followed by an age-appropriate time-out (between thirty seconds and two minutes, depending on the age of your kid and their ability to sit still—make this doable and winnable for them). If she can complete the time-out quietly and follow that with a respectful conversation about what happened, she can re-earn the privilege she lost. Bonnie created the process this way on purpose; it gives both her and the kid a break to collect thoughts, take some deep breaths, and try again. There are other consequences on the list, but Bonnie hardly ever has to advance to those because the calm-down break is a powerful reset for both of them.

So calm your tits! At least calm one of your tits. Bring that calm to activating situations, and then try to *breathe* to keep the calm as long as you can. And when you can't anymore, take a break and calm your tits again.

# Help Kids Find Healthy Coping Skills and Don't Take Them Away

The ability to self-soothe and handle tough feelings or situations is both a lifelong skill and an ongoing process. We all have things that help us feel safer, calmer, and cared for, and we can help our kids find those activities by giving them options and ideas to try.

We can watch what they do naturally and offer them healthy self-soothing as a coping option. We innately seek homeostasis (unless trauma has hacked our ability to do so to bits). You'll see these behaviors in a baby who cuddles up to a trusted person and falls asleep. Or a toddler who, upon finding their favorite toy, shows visible relief on their little face. An elementary kid who always looks for the cat when she's feeling a little sad. An adolescent who video chats with their friends when they are stressed about homework.

As you're watching kids regulate themselves, offer that feedback. It might sound like, "I can see you feel a little more calm now that you've found your stuffy. Your stuffy helps you feel comfortable." And you will see them visibly calm down, have fun, and feel better.

You may struggle to identify those behaviors happening in real time. That's totally normal. If you haven't been able to identify self-soothing behaviors, you can also identify some things that you know help you feel more regulated and offer those as suggestions. A little bit of time in the sun, some alone time, a favorite song, a comfy blanket, writing in a journal; there's a long list of possible comforts. Communicate that these are things to try, not punishments to bear. And they don't have to continue any activity that doesn't help. You're providing a valuable service to help your kids recognize those possibilities and learn to use those behaviors to return to a calm baseline.

You might feel tempted to use your kids' coping skills as leverage to help improve behavior. But coping skills should never be taken away as part of a punishment. Faith tells this story when training parents and other people who work with kiddos. Her son's (Kid #2) anger coping skill was to go outside and throw his football at the big tree in the back. The tree didn't take it personally, and the physical exercise and repetitive movement was an important part of getting himself re-regulated.

At one point they were fighting about something. No idea what, because his 15th year was a series of chaotic moments with brief interludes of calm before the next storm came crashing to shore. Faith and Kid #2 were going at it, and he asked to be excused to go outside. Faith, mad and not done being mad, said "no." Kid #2 reminded her, "Hey, you said if I ever needed to calm down, I could go outside and throw my football at the tree." Bless his head for advocating for himself instead of ramping up more, because he was straight-up, dead-on, right as fuck. He was trying to activate his safety plan, and Faith's job right then and there was to let him.

But first of all, she had to say she was sorry for saying no, and praise him for doing all the right things in that situation. Apologizing to our kids in the ways that adults never apologized to us when we were kids is hugely important in modeling accountability. We have a tendency, as parents, to desperately try to find the things that matter to our kids and use them to leverage the behavioral expectations we have for them. I mean, really. We're trying not to beat their asses . . . and grounding them feels like the same punishment for us as it is for them because then they're stuck in our houses glaring at us. But we have to remember to not take away the shit that helps hold them together. Their sports, their extracurriculars, their quiet time in their room, their music, their tree-and-football routine, even their phones and electronics. We spent all that time helping them curate healthy coping skills and activities to support their positive humaning. Taking that away from them is really fucked because it undermines their ability to self-regulate, which is the whole thing we were trying to teach them to do. We gotta stop that shit. Have a separate set of consequences that have nothing to do with the coping skills you're helping your kid build. Some options for smaller kiddos would be a time-out option or loss of a small privilege like a toy you're gonna keep for a couple of hours and give back. Bigger kiddos can also take the time-out option or be given an extra job around the house.

# Don't Have Power Struggles

You want a more peaceful home, yes? A place where people are respectful, work together, and always replace the toilet paper correctly? Of course you do. Wouldn't that be way easier to achieve if everyone you live with would just do what you say to do already? Of course it would.

But slavish subservience is not the goal. What you're really seeking is a peaceful home where people are respectful, work together, and replace the toilet paper, *and* those people can think for themselves, do things at their own pace, and even have their own way of replacing the toilet paper. (Even though we all know the only way is with the loose end coming over the top, obviously.)

So don't seek out submission. Don't let yourself get wrapped up in winning a battle with your children because you want the victory. We get it; parenting is hard and doesn't necessarily come with a lot of wins. And kids' lives are hard and don't necessarily come with a lot of wins. It's a frequent battle between parents and kids because everyone wants the win, and stubbornness comes in full force. But if you want a peaceful and collaborative home, the goal needs to be finding a way together.

This doesn't mean that you have to acquiesce every time. It does mean taking a less emotional approach in order to focus on and shape the behavior in question. Have you ever had the type of experience where someone else wanted you to do something their way *and* be happy about it *and* properly ashamed for not seeing it or doing it the way they wanted in the first place? The fuck is up with that, are we right? You did what they wanted, but did you need to fall on your sword in the process? That's an experience based in ideas of hierarchy, and we don't want to be preparing our kids to fit into that power structure in other parts of their lives. They need us to show them another way to interact and accomplish tasks.

When it comes to something that might become a battle, take a deep breath. Focus on your end goal and recognize there might be more than just your way of reaching that goal. Let's say you need the compost taken out every day, and you're assigning it as a task for your kid. The goal is getting the stinky coffee grounds and bell pepper stems out of your kitchen, yes? It doesn't really matter if it happens right after school or just before bed. You might have a preference (and obviously that's fine!), but don't power-struggle over something like that, just focus on the end goal of having an empty compost container.

If you're one of those people who has to feel like you've won, work on ways that you and your kid can win together. Bonnie's husband is a champ at this approach, which is: decide for yourself the minimum level of acquiescence you need from your kid to feel like you've won. Then step it up one notch and ask your kid for that. If they agree to that, *bonus*. But with this method, if you need space to negotiate, you've got it.

Avoiding these power struggles is another important aspect of keeping the people in your house emotionally regulated. You'll have fewer arguments and blowups because the overall stress feels lower, and everyone is managing their own central nervous systems and stress responses. That's a valuable skill for life and helps kids build resilience and mindfulness—there's a solid parenting win that actually matters.

# Building Neuroplasticity

Parenting is a constant practice in accepting both change and fuckery. You learn to adapt and compromise because it's complicated to live in this world, all while protecting and nurturing smaller people to live in this world too. When we adapt and pivot in our lives, we can see that reflected in our brains, a process which is called neuroplasticity. Neuroplasticity is one of those complicated-sounding things that really only means our brains' ability to form and/or reconfigure new synaptic connections. And synaptic connections just refers to the way different neurons connect and communicate with each other so we can think and feel and behave. And promoting our ability to be our best selves relies on teaching our brains new strategies around thinking, feeling, and responding.

Neuroplasticity is built by *doing* things, not thinking things. When you see things like "Doing puzzles prevents Alzheimer's," that's what they mean. At least in oversimplified terms.

And here is the part that is gonna make you a little grump with us. We aren't going to just recommend a sudoku book. We're going to encourage a movement plan. Because—bear with us, we're going to get into some science real quick—besides improving neuroplasticity, exercise also has a controlling influence on developing new blood vessels and neuroglial cells (cells that support neurons and synaptic connections without being directly connected to either because they don't have axons and dendrites . . . don't worry too much about what those are). And. *And.* Exercise clears the Amyloid-$\beta$ peptide (A$\beta$) from the brain. A peptide is a short chain of amino acids, and Aβ is best known as the peptide that causes Alzheimer's when it runs unchecked. All of this is just saying exercise is incredibly useful for keeping your brain zinging and reducing inflammation in the background which also keeps your brain zinging.

Faith hates the word exercise. She's not athletic at all. She is, however, active. And can attest that moving her body is far better for her mental health than eating chips and hummus while watching *Blacklist* with her cats. And she had to find movement for joy and fun rather than punitive "exercise" in her own life. The former is what we are encouraging here. This may also be something you do with your kiddos, which is good quality time and also helps you model how self-care works. If going to the gym is your bag, that's great. Go to the gym. But if regular movement is not part of your daily or weekly routine, let's work on that a bit.

If you (or your kiddos) are stuck sitting at a desk for long periods of time, can you add movement to that process somehow by using an under-the-desk peddler, an exercise ball, etc.? If you have a desk that converts to a standing desk, you can add foam floor padding underneath so you can wiggle and move. Or even add a basic treadmill that you can walk on.

Many of Faith's at-home workout stuff is really inexpensive, like a $30 stair-step machine she can use while watching the aforementioned *Blacklist* with the aforementioned cats. She also has an individual little trampoline and a balancing board that she uses for herself, as well as with clients.

Faith also loves yoga and dance and walking outdoors in nature and incorporates a lot of that kind of activity in her life. These are things that are free or quite nearly freely available to us. You can follow yoga sequences on YouTube (Faith called yoga "crabby stretching" with her oldest kiddo . . . they would stretch out their crabbies until they felt better), or put on some music and have a dance break. A cranky parent and a cranky kid can both benefit from a 90-second dance party, right? If it's available to you, maybe a little bit of yard work or light gardening could be added to your movement routine as well. A few pots of flowers or some veggies you and kiddos can work on together will provide light movement and nice pretty green things too. Movement doesn't have to be strenuous to count for this, and it's beneficial to do things like bend, squat, stretch, and walk—whatever movement is achievable with your body and your circumstances.

## Keep Your End Goals in Mind

It's sometimes wild to realize that you're shaping this smaller human into some kind of bigger adult human. But you are doing that! That's a big responsibility, and you want to do it in a goal-focused way. Think about what kind of adult you're producing to give over to the world, and keep that at the forefront of your interactions and discussions. Are you building this kid to be an adult automaton? Or an adult who follows rules and guidelines thoughtfully? Is what you are fighting about something that is going to be a fundamentally defining aspect of their humanity? It might be if we are talking about bullying, or keeping your word, or being kind and empathic.

Those are the fights worth fighting.

It may not be a fight worth fighting if we are talking about broccoli.

Faith was chatting with a client who was fighting with their ex about their son's dinner-time routine. Ex wanted a clean plate. Client had a courtesy-bite rule. Client wasn't getting steamrolled by Kiddo, but also wasn't playing Miss Hannigan, the antagonist from *Annie*. She said to Faith, "When I think about all the things I value and want to see my child grow up to be as an adult, 'good eater' isn't anywhere on that list."

Faith and Bonnie love that perspective. Kiddo needs appropriate nutrition. Kiddo needs to be open to experiences and willing to experiment and challenge himself. Kiddo needs to respect the effort that people put into meal preparation. Kiddo does not need to love roasted Brussels sprouts. And setting up a fight over Brussels sprouts is fertile grounds for resentments at best and eating disorders at worst.

What are your parenting end goals? Is what you're feeling annoyed about in this moment an important step on that path? Or can you show some grace and flexibility and let it go?

# Boundaries All Over the Fucking Place

Kids need boundaries to help keep them safe. You need boundaries to help keep you safe. Kids will push and push; they need to know where the clear limits are. Laying out clear boundaries helps you create reprimands, corrections, and conversations that are productive, instead of feeling violated when someone crosses a boundary you didn't know you had or needed.

Whatever boundaries you set need to be reasonable and clearly stated, and they might need some explanation. For Bonnie, an important boundary is limiting snacks after school. This is hardly arbitrary, but it can seem that way to a four- or five-year-old. So, Bonnie explained to her daughter that snacks after school are fun, but dinner is happening in 45 minutes, and if her daughter eats a bunch of snacks, her tummy won't be hungry, and then she'll act a fool during dinner. It's nicer for everyone to sit down to dinner and feel genuine hunger in their tummies and joy at having food to share.

Does this mean that her kid never pushes that boundary? Hell no. She pushes it pretty constantly because kids are kids and, while they deeply need boundaries, they relish running into them headfirst and doing so repeatedly and with gusto. Even if you understand and expect that interaction, it can be incredibly frustrating in the moment. If the boundary is important to you, you've got to enforce it consistently. If you're inconsistent, your kid will begin to understand the statistics of getting more of what they want. They know if they ask enough times about enough things, you're prone to get worn down and give in. So, even if you would be okay with a snack today, you've got to stick to it to keep the pushbacks to some degree of minimal.

But! You're also welcome to change your mind about boundaries. If you do so, you'll need to communicate both the new expectation and some of your thought process leading up to it. It will probably go over better if you set this boundary at a time that is separate from any pushback you're getting about the boundary. Stick to what you've set originally (as long as that's reasonable and safe), and. in a couple of hours. you can initiate the conversation about changing expectations.

Boundaries don't make you some kind of buzzkill parent. They make you the parent all the kids want to be around, because they know where they stand and what to expect. You're like the cord attached to the bungee jumper.

Conversations about boundaries will be ongoing and fluid. Some boundaries people innately know they need and can be laid out easily. Some boundaries people may not recognize they need until they feel disrespected and realize they need a clear boundary. Sometimes boundaries change over time, based on people's preferences, emotional availability, or changing perceptions of safety. Some boundaries look different for different people in your life. You might be willing to loan out your lawn mower to the neighbor on the right because you trust they will respect your property and boundaries, but the neighbor on the left will get nowhere near your stuff because they don't have the same respect.

Whatever the situation, teach kids to lay out boundaries calmly and kindly, yet firmly. Offer them some language to try, like "I see you want a hug, but I am not in the mood right now," or "You hugged me without asking first, and I felt a little uncomfortable. Please ask first next time," or even "Last time we saw each other I was not in the mood for hugs, but I feel like hugs are okay today. Would you like a hug?" Allow them to practice that language with you so they find something that feels comfortable and authentic. Boundaries that are founded in empathy and are communicated in kindness are very likely to be respected. So one way to keep the conversation about boundaries at the forefront is to be empathetic to your kids' needs.

Boundaries often come into conflict in relationships, and it's important to teach our kids (and remind ourselves) that all boundaries are our everyday expressions of consent. And they aren't always going to match up nicely with how everyone else navigates the world. Having boundaries that are flexible (as opposed to super rigid or super permeable) is a helpful part of that process, as is the empathy mentioned above. There is no magic answer to how to handle conflicting boundaries, but it's amazing what we can resolve when maintaining connection.

The more we can approach our kids with empathy, the calmer our relationships can feel. It helps to put yourself in the place of your kid; think about how it feels to be little and learning and simultaneously sure you are capable of anything while not actually knowing how to do things. When you feel frustrated, imagine how your kid might be feeling and how you wish people would respond to you when you felt that way. If you were learning how to put your shoes on the right feet, how to drive a stick shift in traffic, or how to get all your homework done on time . . . you'd hope for kindness, compassion, and understanding. Think about that and offer it to your kids: "If I were you, I would feel [insert feeling word here], and I would want to know [A, B, and C] before moving forward. What do you need?"

Parenting from a headspace of empathy means being present and thoughtful. It means we avoid default or snarky answers to questions or requests. Take some time to examine your default answers to things.

- What are your default answers?

- What's your motivation for those answers?

- Are you building a respectful relationship with your kids or would you like to make some different moves?

- When you connect with your own feelings and needs, do your decisions feel more authentic?

# Praise the Behaviors You Want to See More Of

Be specific in your praise. Instead of saying "You're such a great kid!" all the time (not that saying that is a bad thing at all), focus on something more specific, like, "You did such a great job bringing your plate into the kitchen without me having to even remind you. I really appreciate that."

This is a core idea of a form of structured, evidence-based therapy called Parent-Child Interaction Therapy (PCIT). It's brilliant with younger kids who have serious behavioral issues. One of the things that it teaches parents to do (using play as the interaction format) is to differentiate labeled and unlabeled praise and use labeled praise as much as possible.

The idea is to use this as a genuine and specific way to praise and build up the actions you want to see. The reason labeled praise is more effective is because people like to know specifics about what we like about them. Unlabeled praise can make kids feel good and loved, which is obviously great! But it's not shown to elicit behavior change the way labeled praise does.

When Faith was training in PCIT, she commented on the fancy way that one of her bonus kids folded the napkins at family dinner: "Wow, that looks really cool. Thank you for taking the time to make the dinner table look so nice for everyone. That was above and beyond your job to set the table." Damned if that kiddo didn't fold the napkins fancy for family dinners for the next two years.

Sometimes praise gets twisted into something snarky, like "Well, look who finally graced us with her presence this afternoon," or "Oh look! He does, in fact, know how to use a washing machine," but that is not an authentic use of praise. It feels bad to people on the receiving end, and it's not at all in the spirit of praising the characteristics we want to see. Yes, we feel snarky sometimes, but that kind of "praise" is really a form of punishment directed at the behavior we want to encourage rather than discourage.

Using authentic, specific praise is a universal tool. It works not just with small kiddos, but also large and smelly ones. It works pretty damn well on adults, too, whether they work with you or live in your house (or both).

# Let Them Voice Their Opinion, Even if They Don't Get a Vote

Let's talk about valuing our kids' opinions, wants, and desires. Because they do have them. And those opinions and desires can be very strong, but you may not know about any of that if you're not inviting kids into the decision-making process in your home.

Faith and her co-parent team would often collect all the kiddos when there was a big family decision to be made and ask for their input. This was always prefaced with the following: "You aren't actually getting to make the final decision. This isn't a family vote type of decision like what desserts to make for Thanksgiving. But we genuinely want to know your thoughts on the subject. They will inform the decision we make, and at the very least, prepare us for your response to them." The benefits are that kids will have some awareness of the decisions being made that impact their lives, it gives them some mental preparation time, and they don't feel like they are being tossed around at the whim of the adults around them.

Sometimes our kiddos had a very good rationale that absolutely influenced the route we took. Sometimes not. But then we could have a proactive conversation about our process. As in "Hey, Kid #2, we totally get why you wanted $X$, $Y$, and $Z$, but we ended up choosing $A$, $B$, and $C$, and here is why."

The decisions we make as parents affect our families as a whole. Sometimes those decisions are mundane and the consequences minor, but everyone in the family has an opinion. It's so easy to ask kids for their input on weekly meal planning, what they want in their lunches, what they want to do on a Saturday. We might not want as much power to go to kids for bigger decisions, like if we should move, or if we should change jobs, or how we should celebrate the life of a loved one who's died. But from the day-to-day to the once-in-a-lifetime decisions, all family members will be affected, and it's respectful to at least ask for input and have those discussions before the adults make the final plan.

Kids don't have a ton of autonomy or control. We drive them places. We buy their clothes. We take them to school. Every action that happens around them affects them and their lives. But they don't necessarily have a lot of power in these areas. And it can feel pretty shitty to feel the effects of decisions in your life that you had little control over and just have to live with. It's unfair to our kids for them to have to feel this as often as they do. Including them in discussions about decisions and changes can go a long way in lessening that feeling of loss of control and lack of influence that already is inherent in childhood. Faith's dad was career military, and she remembers her parents were making the decision about whether he would be stationed in South Korea for a year while the rest of the family stayed stateside, or whether he would be stationed in Germany for three years and bring them with them. Faith has always been a slightly anxious human, but hearing these discussions didn't make things worse; instead, it allowed her time to think about both of those options so she didn't feel steamrolled by their final decision. She had some mental preparation time for both, which felt far less shitty, even at age nine, than receiving decrees from the adult people about what was coming next in her life.

# Believe Your Kids About Their Feelings and Experience

In the process of validating your kids' opinions and wants, you're generally teaching them that what they say and feel is important to you. Another way to validate that is to trust their feelings and internal experiences. We've all experienced things that made us feel icky for one reason or another, and honoring that can be an important part of being safe. When we ask our kids to ignore that experience, either by explicit or implied directions, we seriously undermine their ability to trust their instincts about people, places, and situations.

There is a key difference between feeling "discomfort" and feeling "distress," and sometimes discomfort is a thing we decide to push through, like riding a bike or meeting new people. If your kid is showing or sharing some discomfort, it's your job to validate that and help them learn when to push through or when to back off. Help them get to the bottom of the discomfort rather than just making them do the thing that's got them feeling uncomfortable. Each of us deserves to learn how to listen to our internal voice and we need to be encouraged to believe it. Deciding to go ahead through discomfort relies on the ability to perform a cost/benefit analysis, which is a teachable skill.

Distress can be handled differently. There's almost always significantly more cost than benefit to pushing through distress; it's a stronger reaction, and we have to override a lot of built-in safety features to do so. When you force your kid to hug a relative they don't want to hug just because it makes you uncomfortable to be viewed as impolite, you've sent the message that your kid's distress is something to ignore. You take away their autonomy and ability to honor their instincts. That's a pretty big price to ask a kid to pay already, but you're also priming them for ignoring those instincts in later interactions.

Consider the following:

- How do you recognize distress and discomfort in your own body?

- How do you observe these reactions in your kids?

- How do you differentiate "discomfort" and "distress" for yourself?

- What are some times you were asked to do something even if it caused you distress?

- How do you feel when you think about those examples?

- How can you talk about this idea with your kids as toddlers? Children? Teens? Adults?

# Let Your Kids into Your Common Living Space

In the same vein as building feelings of influence and autonomy, the idea of sharing your common living spaces is powerful. Kids got added to your established life, right? To make physical space for them, not just in their bedrooms but in other areas of your home, is to make emotional space for them in your life. This is a subtle way of showing your kids that they belong in your home and your life, they aren't just people who live here because state law has determined that's the plan.

Let your children claim space in common living areas. This doesn't mean letting the fucking contents of their toy chest throw up on your living room carpet. It means letting them discuss art and art placement and letting them have their own tchotchke space as well. Faith had a friend with a display cabinet who left the bottom shelf empty for her girls. They were allowed to use that shelf (the reachable one for them) to display whichever of their toys and lovies were important to them, in the same cabinet where mom displayed hers.

We love this. *Love this.* Having their art in shared spaces gave Faith's kiddos an appreciation for art and made them far better at caring for the space. Her son reminded her frequently, "Don't forget, that's mine and it's going with me," about pieces in the house. And upon moving back home recently, he liberated the art he wanted for his room. They have similar taste so shit's gonna get real when he buys a house next year!

The more welcome your kids feel in your home, the more they feel they belong there, the more calm and attached they will feel. That emotional safety can go a long way for all of you to avoid losing your shit on each other.

There's power in feeling influence over your physical surroundings. It feels good for our opinions to be sought out, heard, and valued. Something as simple as, "Do you like this family photo in this frame or that one?" is a minor question, but kids feel good when we solicit their opinions. When people ask what we think, we feel included and like we belong. What a small effort on our part to create big value for our kids.

- What are the areas of your home and physical surroundings that you could change up with a kid's help?

- Are you comfortable with the idea of sharing that creative process with them?

- What boundaries do you need as an adult to make that a fun and engaging experience?

# Communicate Clearly

So many conflicts are born of miscommunication. Communication is fucking complicated. Have you thought about what it means to have a conversation with another person? Your brain creates a series of electrical impulses and thinks of a thing to say, and it sends that thing through a series of filters (your experiences). Then, you say it out loud to another person who hears it, and their brain converts it into a series of electrical impulses, and then proceeds to take it through their own unique filters and wow. It's pretty impressive that we have any interactions without miscommunications.

Add to that basic communication exchange the processing it takes to form a thought. In milliseconds, your brain can catalog thousands of memories and experiences and come up with a takeaway message to share with someone else. That processing is internal, invisible, and quick. That's why sometimes Bonnie has whole conversations with herself in her head before coming to a conclusion, which is the part she says out loud. So here she is, driving along and thinking some big thing, but the only part that is said out loud is something like, "Oh, of course it was the turtle all along," and all the other people in the car are like, "What the fuck are you talking about?" because they weren't privy to all the processing that came before, making that statement seem out of context. Obviously she's talking about some key takeaway from a trip to the zoo, keep up people!

So, how does that understanding of processing and communication play into your parenting interactions? Well, it's all fertile ground for miscommunication and hurt feelings. To avoid that, we have to take some of that processing from being solely internal and turn it into something we say out loud so others understand how we got to the punch line.

Take a deep breath before talking with your kids. Use "I statements" like "I like when dirty socks are put away in the hamper and not left on the floor. When I see dirty socks on the floor, I feel frustrated and annoyed. What I need is for everyone to pick up their own socks and put them in the hamper." Statements like this say exactly what you mean, feel, and need.

When giving instructions, focus on one piece at a time. Kids are learning to operationalize tasks that you take for granted, like how a person needs both socks and shoes to go play outside. Kids need stepwise instructions for stuff like that: "First, you need socks, okay? Tell me when you've got some ready." Cut your communication into smaller, more manageable chunks to help set everyone up for success.

Help your kids find the right words, too. When her toddler was in full freak-the-hell-out mode, Bonnie would say, "I hear you feeling really overwhelmed now. Take a break and we will talk when you're ready to use your words." Stay close by, so they know you're not abandoning the big feelings in the room, and then let them regroup and try again. Self-regulation is an important part of clear communication and involves being able to control your big feelings enough that you can use your voice. It's a skill we have to learn from others.

This type of clear communication is necessary for one of the key pieces of parenting, which is attachment. Attachment is a deep and real connection we feel with another person; it's a relationship of safety, security, and reliability. Attachment requires empathy, compassion, honesty, and vulnerability. Secure attachment helps people manage tough experiences and loss with more resilience. It's built, like trust, with small, frequent actions.

Let's mangle a metaphor, shall we? Think of attachment like a quilt you're making together with your kids. Each stitch, each square, makes the quilt stronger, bigger, and more comfy. Those stitches are made from compassion, clear communication, integrity, and real, deep love. Your quilt keeps your kids (and you) feeling secure and cozy even when storms are knocking around the windows. Your quilt is made from quality materials and can travel with your kids to any place they choose to go. They can choose people to add to their quilt party, too. Over time, the quilt becomes even softer and warmer; it's a touchstone of your lives together.

If clear communication helps you stitch the quilt, unclear communication puts holes in it. Harsh, aggressive, or thoughtless communication makes your quilt less warm and durable. It's not completely avoidable to have some holes; everyone has a missed stitch sometimes. And clear communication can be used to patch up and repair those holes. Attachment thrives between people when there are early and effective repair attempts when something goes wrong. Effective repair reflects how well we can come back together after a freakout; clear communication makes these attempts more successful, more often.

What does effective repair look like? Some common components of repair include (1) a chance for everyone to share their feelings, (2) a chance for everyone to feel validated in their experience of the conflict, (3) a chance to identify and share triggers that may have contributed to the conflict, (4) a chance for everyone to take responsibility for their role in the conflict, and (5) time for planning how things can go differently next time.

For example, Bonnie and her daughter frequently get heated while cleaning the kid's room. It usually starts as a small spark and can turn quickly into a big fire. Sometimes they yell at each other and then need to retreat to different rooms to cool off; they both can feel disoriented by how quickly these exchanges can escalate, even though it happens repeatedly. No matter how many times they go through it, they still engage in a repair conversation when they've cooled off. That typically sounds like Bonnie saying something like, "I feel sad that we got angry so quickly about something small. I think you felt frustrated that I was telling you how to make the bed, so you were ignoring my suggestions. That's a trigger for me because I really don't like to feel ignored. I wish I had asked for a break before I started yelling at you, and when this happens again, I will ask for a break."

In most long-term relationships, certain conflicts resurface perpetually, meaning people will cycle through the conflict many times over the course of the relationship. It might look different or be set off by different scenarios, so the goal is to continually get better at recognizing the conflict for what it is and/or initiating repair conversations more quickly.

Repair is so important because something like a fight about making the bed is not worth allowing significant resentment to linger. Let's return to our quilt metaphor. Unresolved conflict, even over something small, can leave rips and burns in your quilt. Keeping repair as a key part of the cycle of conflict lets your quilt get warmer and softer because you've patched the wounds. Ignoring repair makes your quilt threadbare and holey, and when you or your kid reaches for it in a time of need, the fabric won't have the integrity to last. Show respect to your kids and the relationship you're building together by being vulnerable enough to work through the repair process. Attachment thrives when there's room for mistakes to be both made and repaired.

People who are deeply connected and attached to one another will not fight to win. They will fight to understand each other better. When you're in conflict with your loved ones, can you take that approach?

- What are some ways you and your kids are making your quilt?

- Are there holes that need your attention?

- How can you make your quilt bigger and more comfortable?

- What changes to your communication approach are you willing to make?

- What will your repair language sound like?

# Find Your Love Languages

Gary Chapman's book *The 5 Love Languages* is one of those huge bestsellers with a zillion spin-offs, and for good reason . . . it's a really good model for looking at how we communicate love. Love isn't a feeling after all. It's a behavior.

Now, the book is heteronormative, gendernormative, and Judeo-Christian, with scripture quotes. We say that with the caveat that we know most of us don't fit neatly in all (if any) of those categories. Faith admits that she's totally hacked

Chapman's online love language quiz when using it in groups to be more inclusive. If you decide to take the quiz, you may have to do the same thing in your mind.

But, anyway, digression. The point is we all have ways that we express love and wish to receive love. Chapman refers to these categories as: (1) acts of service, (2) quality time, (3) touch, (4) words of affirmation, and (5) gifts. Faith loved discussing these categories with her kiddos. They loved being asked about their love languages. And it helped shape their parent-child relationships in positive ways.

Now, Faith's son (Kid #2) *says* that gifts are his love language. And the dude likes getting shit. Which is all good. But his real love language? Words of affirmation. He thrives on praise. And needs to be praised for something more than once to reinforce it for him. And it's really important to remember that when she's all "Buddhadamn, I'm busy, child . . . go away." But praising him fills his love cup and helps reinforce his positive behaviors. Win-win.

Most people take the Love Language quiz and say, "What the fuck? I don't want to have to choose just one of these!" You're not choosing just one. You're focusing on the one that lands the deepest for you so you can clearly communicate that experience to others. And it gives you a way to ask others about their experience and what lands most deeply for them. It's a beautiful and positive way to build a relationship because you get to say to someone, "I will love you in all these ways, but which way will hit you the hardest?" and then be able to give them a big warm fuzzy feeling of validation and acceptance. That's some good emotional shit right there.

# Learn the Secrets of Therapists

Faith and Bonnie are about to give you something they spent many hours and student-loan dollars in mastering: therapeutic manipulation. "What?" you say, "Manipulation is bad and something that hurts people!" And to that we say "Yeah, most of the time. But not this time!"

Really, all behaviors are manipulative because behavior helps us meet needs. We choose behaviors with the hope that other people around us will respond by meeting our needs, which is not inherently negative or hurtful. Behaviors become negatively manipulative when we attempt to get people to do things *we* think they should do, or things that might hurt them, or things that protect our own egos or interests. Negative manipulation is harmful because it's not done in good faith or with integrity.

Therapeutic manipulation is simply a way to decrease resistance against doing the right thing. It's a way to get people to do the thing that is right *for them* by attaching it to their own value system and approaching it as if it's a done deal. Like:

- "You are so much smarter than I was about these kinds of things at your age. I know that I don't even need to tell you that you should . . ."

- "Some people would just . . . but I know you don't roll like that and are going to handle it by doing . . . or . . ."

- "Did you notice they handled that in a way that was pretty selfish? Like doing . . . ? I'm so glad you don't act like that!"

Therapeutic manipulation is meant to be thoughtful and empathetic because it requires knowing someone pretty well to use it effectively. You have to know a person's value system and what they are likely to do in situations in which their values are called upon. You have to use it sparingly because, "With great power comes great responsibility, Peter Parker Parent."

This is parenting tai chi, y'all. Faith has both used and taught this technique with many clients and one of those clients told her, "I loved how you totally got me to do the right thing without once directly telling me what to do or how shitty I was for not wanting to do it right off the bat." So even when we know what's happening, we still respond well to that kind of dialogue.

# Work to See Your Kids the Way Other People Do

We know you love your kid. Bonnie will admit she's straight-up obsessed with her kid. But we spend a lot of time with those kids and they don't always bring their A game. They are grouchy and hangry, and they talk back and leave their shoes on the stairs even though we've told them 60 bazillion times not to do that. And because our brains pay a lot more attention to negative stuff (thanks negativity bias) it's easy to start to feel that negative energy seeping into your interactions.

So it can feel jarring at times when you go to parent-teacher conferences and the teacher is like "omg your kid is such a joy to have in class! They are helpful and respectful and they never make a mess!" and you're in your head like, *But that little hooligan just spilled red Kool-Aid all over my back seat!* It's jarring because it brings up complicated emotions for us as parents. We want to feel the swell of pride we get when we hear things like that about our kids. We want to believe we are raising exactly that kid who is helpful and kind and thoughtful about shared spaces. And we may also feel a little envious that the teacher gets these interactions and we rarely do. Or we may feel confused about how our experiences can be so different. We get wrapped up in the day-to-day stressors and we forget all the things that make them great. Seeing their good qualities through fresh eyes helps decrease overwhelming feelings, discontent, and resentment and helps us see our parental successes. It's a good reminder about how your hard work is paying off, even when it doesn't seem like it.

And! Often, your kid puts on their best behavior for other people, right? So when you look through someone else's eyes, you're seeing the topflight abilities of this kid you're in the trenches with at home. It's a refreshing perspective and an excellent reminder that you're raising a kid you *want* to see interacting in the world. You can use the knowledge of their best abilities as fuel for your clear communication and focused, authentic praise.

Reassure yourself that your kid shows you their toughest behavior because they trust you to handle it maturely and safely; they feel secure enough to act like a turd. You can hold both of those extremes for them because all of those pieces are true. Our kids are turds, and they are star students, and they are expert mess-makers, and they do trust us to give them space for all of those experiences. Your job is to make space in your mind for the ways other people see your kids' strengths and assets.

# Validate the Choices Your Kids Make and Help Them Learn from Mistakes

Remember when we talked about building your capacity for self-compassion? Now's your chance to show your kids how to build theirs! Making mistakes is a common human experience, and we all need a way to process our missteps with more encouragement and less shame. If we expect perfection from our kids, we will stymie their ability to practice or try new things or to take accountability when mistakes happen. Don't forget that self-compassion pushes us toward betterment and more achievement because it focuses on effort and journey rather than perfection. However, if no one is perfect, it becomes easy to give up when we struggle. So take what you've learned in your self-compassion journey and model it for your kids, so hopefully, they cultivate supportive observers earlier than you might have found your own.

Sometimes, our kids choose things that we wouldn't have chosen or that we maybe don't think are a great idea. And then they do those things anyway and it turns out great! And our human impulse is to be all, *Well, look at you; everyone gets lucky sometimes*, in a bitter voice. But try this instead: "I didn't think that would have worked, but you did a great job; it looks great!" because this says to your kid: *Look at you! You knew yourself, you made a good choice based on that knowledge, and you were more right about this than the powerful people in your life!*

That can be a hard one, because we've known our kids for a long time. We've guided them and watched them grow. We've supported them based on what we thought was best with the best information we had at the time. So when our kids go rogue . . . whew. That's a tough space because we've made it this far on the fuel of our own adult assuredness. But we've also been modeling that assuredness for our kids, and they need to know that they can trust their instincts, too.

Real talk: sometimes those choices are bad as hell, or even dangerous or problematic, or maybe the choice wasn't bad but it still didn't work out for them. How can we validate those choices for our kids using this model? Remember that all of our failures are training grounds. Use those chances to say to your kid, "I wouldn't have picked that for you for many reasons. You tried anyway and maybe you don't feel great about the outcomes. What have you learned about yourself from this experience?

What do you want to try differently next time? What were some of the factors that guided you toward this decision?"

These types of conversations require empathy and compassion; your tired, frazzled parental heart is big enough to hold those feelings along with anger or worry about the situation. Approaching it with compassion can help everyone process shame in a way that is constructive instead of entrenching.

Sometimes their decisions have serious consequences and they will need your support to manage the outcomes. You still want to aim to validate the process they used to make the decision and help them identify spots where they might have made a different move. As in "I know how much you care for and love your friends. I see why you thought lying for them was a good way to show them love by protecting them from consequences. But it ended up causing them more issues in the long run because the situation was far more dangerous than either of you realized."

We all make decisions all the time that have unintended or unforeseen effects. Kids will need your guidance in taking responsibility for their role and for the ways they can contribute to repairing damaged property or relationships.

A reminder too about brain development. The parts of our brains associated with planning ahead and imagining consequences don't come fully online until around the age of 25. There's somewhat limited brain ability to complete some of these cognitive tasks, and even the most mature young person needs additional adult guidance through decision-making processes. Just because they look grown and talk grown doesn't mean they don't need your input, so stay involved and inquisitive in their decisions.

Turns out, both parents and kids are humans. And humans fuck up. Like, a lot. Mistakes and failures are the chances we are given to grow, if, that is, we take time to acknowledge and learn from those mistakes. This means we are straightforward and honest about the ways we've messed up. It means we don't try to hide, deny, or cover up behaviors that are hurtful.

It means we say to someone supportive, "This happened and I feel like shit about it. Can you [help me, forgive me, guide me, love me anyway]?" If we as adults take this approach, it will become the default for our kids. What a beautiful way to build resilience, kindness, and humility that also builds trust and strength in your parent-offspring relationship.

Mistakes are chances to repair, to mend, to make your relationships stronger. But to make a mistake can feel icky. To acknowledge that mistake, to yourself or others, can take a lot of courage. Shame makes us tempted to cover up or ignore a mistake in the hopes that no one else will see our misstep.

Your job is to take a deep breath, acknowledge any defensiveness you feel, and turn your compassion on full blast. Your ability to show emotional vulnerability will make your relationships more elastic and resilient overall.

Perfection is something people believe they want, but really, perfection is boring. "Perfection" is a white-lady Instagram influencer doing a tree pose in front of a sunset—a snapshot that omits the subsequent loss of equilibrium and the ungainly squawk that burbled from her throat. It's not interesting, it doesn't challenge anyone, and it's an incomplete picture. Think of the people in your life you love to spend time with the most. We would wager they are far from perfect; they are awkward and vulnerable and bad at parallel parking.

They bring challenges and mistakes, and they are interesting! Bonnie works with a lot of clients who have anxiety, and it's often rooted in perfectionism and the shame that comes with mistakes. During one session, a client was processing some of these feelings and said "I think maybe perfect is like uncooked flour. It looks unblemished but no one wants to eat it." Is that not the coolest simile ever?

# Give Feedback Like a Pro

A lot of clients come to therapy with the goal of managing perfectionism or because they have a lot of anxiety around taking feedback or criticism. Many of us, when we were kids, were not approached with empathy when it came time for feedback, and we formed protective coping skills to avoid those interactions because they felt icky. We either strived for perfection so we could be above criticism, or became good at hiding mistakes so we could avoid criticism.

Those behaviors were important to help us feel safer, but as adults, it's limiting to be fearful of feedback. We have to do a lot of emotional work to untangle our fear and shame responses from those childhood experiences. As we begin to parent our own kids, we want them to have a different experience of feedback and critique.

When Faith was training to be a board supervisor, her professor taught the class to give feedback in the following format: positive, positive, negative, positive. And if it works with grown-ass people with graduate degrees, maybe kids could benefit from not being negged out all the time as well, eh?

The idea is simple. Kiddo is sent to clean their room. When you go to check on them, you see they have maybe not done the very best job, even though they know your expectations and you told them how to do it. You might want to get sarcastic or snarky, but let's try this feedback approach: "You did a great job getting all the laundry put away, and I like how you organized all the books on your desk, I bet that will make getting homework done easier! The floor still needs to be swept, but the clean sheets on your bed look great, so I think you're nearly done!"

This works far, far better than saying, "Did you lose the fucking broom?" And your kid is all, "No, I just couldn't get to it cuz you have it stuck up your ass again!" Aaand now all peace treaties are off.

Yeah, the professor's approach can be a pain in the broom-filled ass. Especially when you have to be creative in finding the positives. But Faith swears it has canceled out so many potential arguments at Casa Harper, it's well worth the expenditure of emotional energy!

We all have scripts we use for interactions like this. What are your scripts and where did they come from?

- Are you a recovering perfectionist who struggles with feedback? Are you too critical of your kids' attempts at new things? Are you giving feedback that lands harshly? Or are you avoiding giving feedback altogether because of your own experiences with it?

- Are you giving feedback in a way that can be heard and integrated, or do people around you shut down when you try to share these ideas with them?

- Are you building your relationship by offering growth areas compassionately?

If your scripts aren't serving your family relationships, it's time for a rewrite.

# MAKE HEALTH A FAMILY VALUE

*T*his chapter is about caring for the bodies that carry us through life. It's about being a whole-ass person instead of a half-ass person. It's about taking good care of yourself so you have energy to take on bigger issues and ideas. Burnout and stress are very real challenges in parenting when you're also trying to live your life and fight for whatever you believe in. And all that stress affects your health in real and serious ways. Our brains and bodies are not very good at managing stress long-term; we are mainly made for quick fights or fast getaways. Long-term stress creates inflammation, and inflammation like that is linked to hundreds of ongoing disease processes. So, you've got to create a base level of taking good care of your physical, mental, and emotional health.

## Connect with Your Own Body and Teach Your Kids to Connect to Theirs

Talk with your kid about trusting how they feel physically. If they are sick, or have a headache, or just need more rest, this is all part of knowing our own health and being responsible for it. Questions like "How do you feel? Where does it hurt? Is your heart beating faster than normal?" can help even little kids understand that our physiology changes in ways that we cannot see but that are important to feel.

Bonnie's lost count of how many times she has said to her daughter "I think you're doing a little pee dance. Maybe it's time to sit on the potty for a minute?" and heard "No, I do not need to sit on the potty, and also you can't make me because I'm busy!" only to watch her rush to the potty two minutes later in a panic. From very early on, we feel like our physical needs get in the way of the fun stuff. Even as adults, we try to ignore the signals we get from our bodies because, hello, stop interrupting this sweet-ass Netflix binge, body! We have to teach our kids that meeting those physical needs and listening to our bodies is an important part of staying connected to and honoring our bodies and the ways they serve us.

One of the most powerful ways you can take care of your health is by being in tune enough with your physical and emotional feelings so that you can recognize what's happening and make decisions based on those cues. Are you hungry or thirsty? Are you achy and need a quick stretching session? Are you sleep deprived or otherwise fatigued? Do you need to pee? Do you need to hear the sound of a good friend's laughter?

Slow down, take a few deep breaths, and ask yourself what you feel and what you need. Our brains can get overwhelmed and overloaded, and then they overheat and crash like an old iPhone. The process of taking a few deep breaths can turn down the heat, so to speak, and remind you that you've got the power to turn down the fire alarms clanging in your head.

When we are stressed and activated, powerful chemicals are released into our brains, and if we make decisions in that headspace, they are likely to involve a lot of dickitude. You know in *Frozen* when the trolls sing that song about being a fixer upper? There's a line that goes, "People make bad choices when they're mad or scared or stressed! Throw a little love their way and you'll bring out their best!" Those damn trolls are really onto something.

We all, kids and adults, need a go-to calm down approach. Deep breathing, stretching, time-out in another room, a soft blanket or toy, a step outside, a quick blast of our favorite music, cuddle time with a pet . . . there are lots of safe options that can work. Try a bunch of things and see how you feel. Help your kids try a bunch of things and see how they feel. Connect with your own breath and love and don't jump into the fray when your brain is in redline panic mode.

If you need help identifying some coping skills that might work for you, Faith and Bonnie invite you to (maybe, possibly?) therapy. They know that sometimes people feel squeamish about therapy, or don't know what to expect from it. But Faith and Bonnie think of therapy as a place where you can learn tons of new, weird coping skills to help you connect with, and regulate your body and emotions. You can learn those skills without ever talking about anything too painful or scary. And if you learn something new and weird and you're into it, isn't that great? Faith and Bonnie have both been therapists with therapists. Not everything is deep, right? Sometimes it's nice to have the perspective of someone not living in that situation at that moment who doesn't have a relationship with you in another facet of life. Seriously, Faith loves being able to say, "Is this as fucked up as I think it is?" and her therapist saying, "Yes, totally," or "Nah, not really. Have you had anything to eat in the past couple of hours, Admiral Hangry?"

# Reward Hygiene

Bodies are places where a lot of germy things happen, they stink if you don't clean them and cleaning them properly is a process.

Hygiene can be a battlefield because it's a place where the kid has all the control, and they fucking know it. And even if they know that it's a good idea to brush their teeth, they know that adults can't really force them to do it, and man, do they go on little power trips over that. For some kids, a reward chart can help decrease the bedtime war games. So, like, a little sticker chart with all the things they need to do, and they get a prize when they get a week's worth of stars or whatever. This works for lots of kids, but not all kids. It's okay to try a few things to maximize the motivation that works in your home, and then you can stop yelling/begging/cajoling at bedtime. Also, note that you may need to reassess your motivation system occasionally. When Bonnie's kid was younger, the sticker chart totally worked. As time passed, the stickers lost their significance. The family has pivoted several times since; get creative and see what works in your family.

Talking about hygiene can seem near impossible with older kids who already think you are stupid af and need to stay out of their lives. Faith's kids were both pretty reasonable about hygiene, but when issues became apparent (cuz no one's perfect), she tied in a reward system the same way Bonnie has for her kid.

They wanted cute clothes? Those clothes had to be taken care of, which included not stinking them the fuck up. Replace cute clothes with gray sweats for a week and hygiene improves pretty fucking fast, trust Faith. She also would have them be part of the hygiene product purchasing process, noticing they were far more likely to use stuff they picked out over the stuff that the Mommy Fairy just left in the bathroom. She also tried (and gets a gold star for this one) to praise good hygiene when it happened instead of pointing out bad hygiene when it didn't.

And if bad hygiene needed addressing, it was done with humor and a presumption that it was unintentional. Like, "Dude, you smell like ass banana, practice must have been rough today! I'll hold dinner so you can grab a quick shower before we eat!" Faith would also try to head off possible hygiene issues at the pass by planning ahead of time. Like, "Dude, I know you are spending the long weekend playing video games with your cousins in the pit of despair known as your cousin's bedroom. I need to pick you up at 3:00 p.m. for family dinner, so make sure you give yourself time to scrub off the pizza sauce, hantavirus, and general stank, and put on clean clothes before I get there, cool?"

# Navigate Diet Culture Without Shame

Were you raised by a Boomer? Boomers as a generation have been exposed to more toxic messages about diet, food, and weight than any generation before or since. And if you were raised by a Boomer or had lots of contact with them, you've likely absorbed lots of that toxic sludge for yourself. Diet culture is capitalism at its ickiest. It thrives on the idea of some "ideal" or "default" body, and those of us who don't have one of those ideal bodies better (1) feel really shitty about not being ideal, (2) try to manipulate our bodies into being ideal, (3) spend lots of money, energy, and time on that manipulation, and (4) make sure other people feel as bad as we do if they don't meet the ideal.

Gross. That's definitely not the message we want our kids to get from us, simply because we haven't unpacked it for ourselves, nor from grandparents or other Boomer adults in their lives. Diet culture is a swampy place that breeds lots of disordered eating, shame, and depression. How are you going to make sure you're not dragging your kids into that swamp with you?

Start by noticing you're in the swamp.

- What messages are you getting every day about your body or other people's bodies?

- Are you following diet culture influencers on social media?

- Are you constantly talking about food or your body with other people?

- Who benefits from the ways you're talking about your body?

- What do you hear other people saying about food or bodies?

Keep unpacking and questioning the ways you have been indoctrinated to feel shame.

As you start to realize the ways diet culture affects you and your relationship with your body, we invite you to aim for a space of feeling neutral. Diet culture teaches us to hate our bodies, to feel shame or even disgust about them. Those are feelings that won't go quietly into the night, so try to be neutral about your body. It's maybe not realistic to love every inch of your body every day, but neutral is safe territory. From neutral, we can go to gratitude for the ways your body lets you interact with the world. We can be thankful for strong arms for hugging, or loud voices that can sing David Bowie karaoke in the car.

Make some rules for yourself and other adults for talking about bodies, food, and weight around your kids. Ideally, all the adults will be in neutral-to-grateful territory. They will avoid labeling foods "good" or "bad" and they will avoid those labels for themselves when they eat. ("I'll be good and eat the salad." "I feel so bad when I can't resist the bread basket!")

The diet and weight loss industry is a big moneymaker and a key part of the economy. The messages are strong, pervasive, and ubiquitous. The industry took a bit of a hit during the pandemic, and then we all watched it come back stronger and more aggressively than ever.

Bodies are not something to be fixed. They are something to be cared for thoughtfully, talked to nicely, and lived in fully.

If you notice your kid starting to talk about their diet or body in these terms, try to assess where these feelings are coming from. Have they recently started spending time with different people or consuming different media than usual? Are they on the verge of physical changes like puberty? How's their overall mental health? Because diet culture is in fact so insidious, it can sneak in from a lot of angles. It's also possible you'll want the support of a professional like a therapist or dietitian.

# Enjoy All Foods in Moderation

When Bonnie was raising a toddler she often joked about how eating with a toddler is sort of like eating with a snake—they want to eat one type of food, in huge amounts, on Tuesday, and then not really eat again until sometime next week. Threenagers, for real.

In general, however, as our kids grow, leading them into moderation is key. Bodies need nourishing food all the time, and there are many ways to get that food, whether your family is vegetarian or gluten-free or dealing with nut allergies. It's about balance and moderation with no shame or guilt.

Moderation means listening to your hunger signals and figuring out the difference between real hunger signals and emotional hunger signals. Giving your body time to send the "full" message to the brain before eating a second helping . . . and then deeply enjoying that second helping if you are truly not full.

Faith had the hardest time for years with grocery shopping. Whatever treats she would buy would be all devoured within two days of going to the store. Which left everyone five days of nothing but carrot sticks. She started talking about it in terms of math with her kids. For example, saying there were enough granola bars for them to have one each day when they came home from school. She wouldn't yell at them for having two, but there wouldn't be one available on day seven if they did so. This approach deflated the snack wars, and her kids moderated *themselves* way better because doing so was now their choice.

Further, our kids need to know that we are not good or bad people because of what we eat. Like, you're not superior because you skipped out on a brownie when someone else didn't. Being extremely restrictive with foods can breed an environment for binging. As long as everyone is eating nourishing food most of the time, indulging can happen free of guilt, and it doesn't mean anyone is weak. Bonnie talks with a lot of clients who say things like, "I feel like a bad person when I eat bad foods." No one's humanity or goodness is dependent on the ability to resist Girl Scout cookies. And foods aren't inherently bad for existing. Especially Girl Scout cookies. Some foods taste better. Some foods are better at helping our bodies work their best. Both are good things based on different goals.

If you find yourself in patterns of eating that could be disordered or overly emotional, you're not alone in that at all. Because of diet culture, we've all been trained to be on one plan or another for most of our lives. Take some time to consider what you eat and why you eat it. Make notes about your emotional connections and relationships to food and eating. If it feels like too much to manage alone, reach out to a friend, therapist, or dietician for additional support. Most people know what it's like to have a complicated relationship with food. Keep a close eye on your kid's eating patterns too. Disordered eating can be easy to hide in teens and college students. Patterns like binging and purging, restriction, avoiding food all day so they can drink alcohol all night . . . these are all behaviors that can become lifelong habits that are then reinforced by our old enemy: diet culture. It's a terrible cycle and we deserve to be done with it.

# Share Healthy Physical Activity

Many of us have a very complicated relationship with exercise, thanks again to diet culture. We may have used it as punishment for eating something, as a way to earn something we want to eat, or as justification for any number of rewards in our lives, and many of us are having to detangle our own hang-ups about exercise as we try to teach kids the value of it.

We may have been shamed about our lack of athleticism. We may have been very athletic and let that part of our lives go as work and family demands on our time have increased. We may feel intimidated by gym culture. Those are all valid reasons we get away from healthy movement. But moving our bodies is an important part of overall health and wellness. It keeps us physically healthy, but can also decrease symptoms of anxiety, depression, insomnia, and distraction. Faith will tell you she considers herself an active person, not an athletic one. This reframing takes the pressure off, and no one laughs at her if she bites it. Usually.

This idea of having a life that is fun and active is in direct opposition to using exercise for punishment (like your middle school gym coach might have done), which is counter to all of those benefits. We can exercise without being trapped on a treadmill for an hour, sweating and cursing the person who told us we needed more exercise; we can hike, bike, dance, walk while chatting, chase butterflies . . . there's a myriad of fun and fulfilling ways to move our bodies.

Kids are, in general, already good at that perpetual joyful motion stuff. Encourage them to keep that up. Playing at the park? Dance party in the kitchen? Definitely movement. If we teach our kids to maintain their joy of being alive in their bodies, we can probably rediscover that for ourselves.

This might mean that you have to drive them to twelve soccer practices per week if that's how they love to move. This might mean that you take a nightly walk around your neighborhood at the end of the day to talk and connect. Bonnie and her daughter often walk the dog together at the end of the day, and it's a time where they joke with each other or talk about serious things and ideas. The important part is reiterating to your child that body movement is not punishment and it does not have to be intense to be beneficial. Talk about how we can find joy in moving our bodies in ways that do not bring us pain, that are appropriate for our abilities, and that we try to do each day.

Movement is a place where we can rise to new challenges (like rock climbing) or something we can practice and improve (like dance). But it's also available to us as simple pleasure.

Think about your relationship with movement:

- What types of movement bring you pleasure?

- What are your feelings about movement and exercise?

- What messages do you want your kids to get about movement?

- How can you make joyful movement a family priority?

Overall, how do you assess your family's connection to physical health and wellness? Taking care of our physical bodies is a key part of feeling good.

# BUILD YOUR COMMUNITY

---

*O*ne of the most powerful gifts you can give your kid is a sense of belonging in community. Community increases our feelings of connection and safety, can improve our physical health, and can provide resources when we struggle.

If you're working for change in any of the areas we talk about in this book, part of the joy of activism is making it a group project.

# Get to Know Your Neighbors

We are becoming more and more isolated in our own communities. No one says you have to go to every neighborhood picnic, but sometimes our safety and well-being comes from a community network.

Bonnie and her family live in a neighborhood that was built in the 1960s. Many of their neighbors are original owners of those homes, and they are the sweetest little elderly ladies in the world. Nosy as hell, but with the best intentions. They watch the house during the day, they bring over little snacks, and they tell stories about the old days in the neighborhood. Bonnie's family met these ladies by walking around to the neighboring houses and introducing themselves when they moved in. They exchanged phone numbers, and then the ladies started bringing the snacks.

One afternoon, one of the ladies fell in her backyard. Her friend with whom she talked on the phone every night couldn't find her, so she came over to Bonnie's house for help. Bonnie's husband went searching and found the neighbor in the backyard, where she had lain for hours. In that situation, the fact that they knew each other was an actual matter of life and death.

Knowing your neighbors means you'll know, and be able to tell your kids, which houses are safe for them to go to if they need help. Emergencies happen, and your kids need a plan to get help from a trusted adult. A good neighbor is a great option for this because of proximity and knowledge of your family.

Teach your kids that neighbors don't have to be our best buddies, but we do owe it to each other to keep an eye out for one another. Show your kids how to be a good neighbor by making polite small talk with neighbors, checking in occasionally, and celebrating holidays with little thank-you cards. You can start by baking some cookies together and then bringing them over and introducing yourselves: "Kidperson and I were on a baking spree. We thought it would be a good time to come over and say hi since we could share the love. Hi! I'm Faith and this is my Kidperson!"

Meet your neighbors. Take good care of them. Let them take good care of you. Faith's claim to fame is that when she bought a new house (two years ago) after living in the same one for 17 years, one of her neighbors sold her house and followed her to the new neighborhood. Not in a creepy stalker way, but in a community-building way. It's also a great neighborhood, to be fair. Make the world safer and friendlier right outside your door.

# Teach Good Hosting Manners

Okay, so you're ready to start your feminist book club and the first meeting is coming up. You're putting yourself out there as a community builder. What an honor, bringing new people together for an exchange of ideas and lots of cheese consumption. You look around and it seems like people are clicking! Conversations are happening! Phone numbers are being exchanged! Cheese is being consumed! Hooray! But wait; here comes your kid like, "Why all these people got their shoes on? We don't wear shoes on the carpet!"

Now the vibe is awkward, and you're going to have a lot of leftover cheese cubes.

We all have day-to-day rules to make our households function more easily, like taking off our shoes at the door to reduce dust (is that just Bonnie that is a total freak about that? Faith says yes, but she has a Roomba so she doesn't have to worry about the dust buildup as much), but those same rules can be really awkward for guests, and our kids need to know the difference.

So, before the next time you manage to get your shit together to host a lovely New Year's Eve party, or clothing swap, or packing-backpacks-for-refugees gathering, discuss the ways you bend or alter your normal house rules to help guests feel welcome. Explaining, "Our friends are showing up, and we will let them keep their shoes on; it's more comfortable for everyone" will hopefully help you avoid the earlier scene.

You can involve kids in hosting from an early age. Inviting friends over to play is great practice. For parties or more organized get-togethers, they can help with invitations, choosing the guest list, cleaning up to make everyone comfy, and choosing and setting out drinks and snacks. Talk in advance about situations that might come up and how to deal with them. Like, what do you do if a guest spills something? How do you ask your friend to leave when you're tired or need some alone time? What if you host a sleepover and your friend wants to go home early? What if your friend isn't respecting boundaries around your things or space? These are relational skills we don't know we need until we need them, so it's helpful for kids to have a chance to practice and feel less awkward about these interactions.

When everyone feels welcome and comfy, the connections can be made and the new ideas can flow.

# Teach Manners for Visiting Other People's Homes

At the same time, we need to talk to our kids about the manners they need for visiting other people's homes. We might make an exception to the no-shoes rule for guests, but another family might not, and that's okay. This is an important lesson in following social cues, asking for guidance, and being a courteous and thoughtful person. We may not always agree with or follow other people's standards, but on their turf we can respect anything that isn't harmful. And learning the customs and traditions of others is a really beautiful way to help broaden our children's understanding of the world and how other people think and interact.

Prepare them ahead of time for what a new situation may be like. For instance, if you're going to a fancy dinner party, you can coach them ahead of time on what silverware to use for each course (start outward, work inward on the silverware lineup); if they're visiting a home with skittish animals, you can use a stuffed animal to help young kids practice asking for permission to give pets and accepting that no might be an answer.

Encourage them to watch what others are doing and self-correct. Coach them to look for visual cues (like a stack of shoes next to each door or a set of coasters on the table) or to ask politely for guidance, "Is it okay to keep my shoes on in here?" or "Do y'all have any coasters? This table is gorgeous, and I don't want to mess it up."

There are boundaries between what feels uncomfortable and what is unsafe. Taking off your shoes might feel awkward but is probably okay. Taking off other clothing is not okay. For kids anyway. At whatever types of parties you adults go to, it's totally fine.

# Understanding Family Cultures and Differences

Not everyone your kid meets is going to have parents who you see eye to eye with. Not everyone your kid meets will even have adequate parents. Part of building community is understanding differences. We want our kids to be kind, thoughtful, and nonjudgmental (when possible) in their interactions with other people's family members. There is a delicate balance here between being kind and holding their authenticity around their own ideas and convictions.

Prepare your kids to be in different environments, for instance, visiting a friend whose family observes a different religion from yours or just lives differently. Some of these things are just differences. For example, if your family isn't Muslim and your kiddo's new friend is, you can explain that she celebrates Ramadan, which is why her family isn't eating during the day right now. You can find resources and teach them about these beliefs and how to respect them. Not all of these differences are just differences, however. Some may lead to disagreements and stronger feelings.

They're inevitably going to meet other people whose values differ strongly from their own, whether that's in dietary choices or expressed biases or religion, or (especially in the South) preferred sportsball team. In fact, that's a good example of things that adults bicker about good naturedly (Spurs or Mavericks? I suppose you could be a Mavs fan if you like being sad and wrong.) and things that shape our culture in ways that are exclusionary instead of inclusionary.

Let them know that you'll support them if they choose to engage in tough conversations with other adults. Remind them to stick to the principles of keeping a level head and a curious approach to tough conversations. Teach them some gentle start-ups, like, "I hear what you're saying, but that hasn't been my experience. Can you explain some more?" Teach them it's okay to walk away from conversations that feel unsafe, judgemental, or aggressively patronizing. We owe it to our brave and passionate kids to cheer for the courage of their convictions, as well as their ability to know when to walk away from adults that can't hear it and can't keep them safe.

# Teach Your Kids How to Make and Maintain Friendships

## Humans Are Built for Connection

Which is why friendship is so extremely important in our lives. Having a good friend has been shown to increase our sense of belonging, lower our stress levels, and improve our overall health. Friends give us a chance to love and to be loved, to feel supported and offer support. Knowing you have a reliable friend makes you feel less lonely and gives you the knowledge that there's always someone in your corner ready to celebrate or commiserate. Friends choose one another and that is a unique bond.

Our kids need ways to cultivate that companionship, and those are skills we all have to learn. The skills required to start a friendship are a discrete set from the skills needed to maintain a long-term relationship, but both sets are rooted in curiosity and confidence. It can be scary to approach a new person and to feel hopeful that they won't reject us. Our kids need the lessons that come with that vulnerability and the payoff that comes with making a true and loyal friend.

So, what are the skills we need to be able to make a new friend? We need to show that we are interested in people and that we can be good listeners. We need to be able to show openness to new ideas and be brave enough to learn something new. We need to go places, initiate conversations, and then be willing to follow up if we meet a person who is open to moving into the early stages of friendship.

To maintain friendship, we need to sustain the effort of checking in and being reliable, and do that long-term. We have to be willing to open up and be our authentic selves, which includes the parts we may have kept quieter in the early stages of friendship. We have to be willing to ask for support and accept it when it's given. And we have to be willing to forgive hurts and repair the relationship when needed.

That may seem like a lot of work to invest, but the dividends are undeniable. Loneliness makes it difficult for us to make meaning in life; we need companions.

Consider the following:

- Who are the friends in your life that mean the most to you?

- How do you recognize a potential friend?

- What are the benefits you get from friendship?

- What kinds of friends do you think are important for your kid?

- How can you support your kid to make and maintain friendships?

Making friends requires an intentional effort; your kids will need guidance about choosing friends and investing that effort.

## When Differences Matter and When They Don't

Diversity is beautiful and happy; the differences that exist between us as far as faith, appearance, or social class shouldn't be a barrier to forming new relationships.However, differences can matter if they relate to safety. We do a disservice to our children when we insist, for example, on being colorblind in a world that isn't. There are situations that they need to be prepared to navigate.

Faith's son has a very dear friend who happens to be quadriplegic and has other medical issues, including a seizure disorder. Her son would want to plan outings for them to do movies, dinner, video games, etc. And that's awesome. But Faith would have to remind him and help him plan around his friend's needs . . . making sure they were going places where he could maneuver his chair, stay out of the sun, and discuss with his friend how to navigate barriers should they come up. (They've been friends for so long, Faith's son will simply pick him up and carry him if he needs to get somewhere that isn't accessible by chair, but not everyone will be down for that.) Does being a quadriplegic matter in terms of him being a good friend? Not a bit. Does it matter when they are hanging out and want to make sure everyone is able to have a good time? Absolutely.

We want our kids to have diverse friends and be accepting of many worldviews. And we can curate that by offering them diverse toys, books, and media to broaden their worldview. There are tons of great books out there about diverse families and relationships. There are books about boys who like sparkly skirts and women who have persisted through sexism. There are movies, TV shows, and songs made for kids which introduce diversity. As Sally Ride once said, "You can't be what you can't see," so seek out diversity for your kids so they value different worldviews and can imagine themselves and their friends in all kinds of jobs and scenarios.

And even though they will choose their own crowd as they age away from us, we can still reiterate certain core values. Our hope is that everyone who hangs out with our kids believes in the universal right to safety; they need to support the idea that everyone's life has value and is worth protecting. If they make exceptions to this, it may mean conversations or setting limits around the time they spend together.

For instance, Faith's oldest kiddo had a friend that was lovely to them (as well as to Faith), but had a tendency to say things that were . . . okay, straight-up racist af. Faith had a convo about it with her older kid, "I know friend-person is really lovely to you and always polite to me, but she also says things that don't align with my values and how I raised you. Something to think about in terms of your interactions with her. And I definitely don't feel comfortable with her being in my home because that could result in other people who have been invited into my home being uncomfortable because of her behavior." Read: "I want my home to be a safer space for people, and I'm not risking friend-person disrupting our peace."

Faith never did well with her parents insisting that any of her friends were shit and didn't want to push that onto her kids. And Faith wanted her kiddo to make thoughtful decisions about relationships and boundaries in their own life. By demonstrating her values in action rather than insisting theirs be the same, she created a thoughtful space where her kiddo didn't feel defensive of their relationships, but instead thought more deeply about them. Hopefully, anyway.

## Time Heals a Lot of Stuff

When Bonnie was a teenager, she remembers having a run-in of sorts with some other girls and feeling really worked up about it. Her dad told her, "You've got to be like a duck and let that dirty water run right off your back." She doesn't remember the specifics of the interaction, because enough time has passed and all of that high school shit gets left behind, but she can remember that guidance and still leans on it in adulthood. The point is, we see our kids hurting in the moment, but we have the wisdom of years to know that all this stuff will pass. We can acknowledge the hurts and injustices without stoking the flames of long-term resentment.

Faith's mom used to say, "They can fuck you over, but only you can fuck you up." (Faith realizes these stories make her mom sound like a crazy, chain-smoking, whiskey-slamming telephone operator as played by Bette Midler. Faith's mom would have you know she never smoked.)

In the moment, when our kids' feelings are hurt or they are upset about a bad grade, we can help them differentiate if their response means that something legit went down that needs to be addressed or if they are just butthurt on general principle. Knowing how to figure out the difference is an important skill. Teach them they can take a step back, take a deep breath, and create the space they need to think about what has happened. Sometimes something hurtful needs to be addressed in the moment or soon after; other times it might be better to say "fuck this noise" and move on. Faith tells all her clients, not just the young ones: "You're not responsible for your first thought. They're called automatic for a reason and are the product of all your experiences. You are responsible for your second thought and your first behavior."

This reminds us to be proactive instead of reactive. Which means learning discernment about how to handle certain issues. Often, the passage of time itself makes hard things easier to bear. Grief over a death or loss, sadness over a miscommunication or lost friendship, anger over a bad grade or harsh feedback from a coach . . . the impact of these lessens with time and support. Other hurtful scenarios call for forgiveness. Forgiveness does not mean allowing continued horrible behavior. It means letting shit go so you can move on. It's like the old saying, "Holding on to anger is like holding on to hot coals and expecting the other person to get burned." There is far more power in just being done than in continuing to spend so much time and energy on being angry.

The world is an incredibly angry place. Anger is an approved emotion in most industrialized, western nations. Our kids internalize that at a preconscious level, which means we have to be highly conscious in our strategies to help them recognize and wield anger appropriately.

# RAISING INCLUSIVE KIDS

*W*e would wager that since you're here, you're already somewhat out of the dominant paradigm. You're here because you want a different world and you're rejecting some of the traditions and beliefs that got us here.

What is the dominant paradigm of family and parenting? It's the outdated 1950s version of family that doesn't serve our twenty-first century needs. It's cishet parents (a matched immutable binary set of one man and one woman, of course) and cishet kids, and probably everyone is white, and definitely everyone is neurotypical, and there's not a lot of space for variation.

If you're outside the dominant paradigm, you're probably already talking to your kids about it. They see differences and feel discrimination and have likely brought it up to you in some way. You've talked about code-switching and other ways to stay safe, and you've worried about your kids in ways other parents haven't. Parenting is already heavy stuff; you've carried even more of the load. We hope that you have a good community of support from other parents outside the paradigm. And we hope some of those dominant-paradigm parents see what you're doing and work to take on some of your load.

If you're in the dominant paradigm, your job is to disrupt it.

- What about you or your family makes you different?

- What are places or relationships in your life where those differences are celebrated?

- What are places and relationships in your life where those differences are seen as deficits?

- How are you disrupting the status quo, and how can you bring more people to that disruption?

There is so much discussion about privilege and what that means. And for every discussion about the recognition of privilege, there is three times as much discussion pushing back against the idea. And privilege, in current discourse, is not "raising seven figures of start-up capital from family and friends" type privilege.

Privilege in this case means *the absence of barriers.* Stairs are not a barrier for anyone who doesn't use a wheelchair (or a different mobility support) or who lives with a chronic pain condition. We don't float magically up them, but we are able to use our legs to move up them without causing harm to our bodies. And this is true of poverty, racism, colorism, sexism, heterosexism, cissexism, etc., etc.

We are trying to see, and help our kids see, things that are so pervasive they become invisible. It is our entire environment. We are not asking fish to watch for the shark. We are asking fish *to become aware of the ocean itself.* This is incredibly difficult, and it's incredibly necessary for the creation of a better society.

This means teaching our kids to believe what other people tell us about their experiences of the world, and to look at the world through someone else's eyes to the extent that they can do so. How do we see the water and teach our kids to see the water? We start with the small things that we can do in the immediate present to give our kids a sense of accomplishment and purpose, like: "Wow, all these carts left all over the sidewalk would make it impossible for someone who uses a walker or is pushing their baby in a stroller to get through. Let's move them to the corral so they are out of the way."

You've just taught your kid to notice that how they maneuver around obstacles isn't possible for everyone. They are going to be less likely to leave their own cart on the sidewalk and make sure that others have as clear a path as possible.

Dismantling these structures when all we have is a plastic spoon is doable if we all start digging away chunks of the foundation with all of our individual spoons.

# Work on Your Shit

We would wager there are few among us who were truly raised to be aware of and confront our own biases. Our families are as varied as we are, and each family does the best they can with what they've got. And, believe it or not, working on your biases requires a similar skillset to many other aspects of parenting. The coping skills needed for examining your own internalized homophobia, for instance, are similar to the ones needed to stay calm while your sixteen-year-old is telling you about the fender-bender they just caused, and both situations are vital to address.

Particularly in the U.S., we are all products of a pretty toxic culture based on fear, scarcity, conformity, and misinformation. A culture that supports ideas of "bootstrapping" and meritocracy, and thinks of differences as something to be mocked instead of celebrated. Stuffing down our feelings, having disordered eating, and body image are also normalized. Being busy all the time. Needing to do everything perfectly and be right all the time. Keeping it a secret when others hurt us. Putting the appearance of cheerfulness and positivity above the hard work and conversations we need to have.

Because we all breathe this toxic air, sometimes we breathe it back out. So if you weren't raised to actively question yourself and your beliefs, you might be breathing out those toxic fumes more often than you realize. You might be acting in ways that are hurtful to others, even if your intention is to cause no harm. You may be planting some of these ideas in your own kids' brains because you're not questioning parts of your identity or belief system.

Maybe you are someone who manages anxiety very effectively through exercise. Your kiddo is advocating for a 504 plan at school and wants to talk to the family doctor about starting medications to help them better manage their anxiety during testing season, and that exercise alone isn't mitigating the issue for them. Your concern is that they won't have this level of scaffolding when they are working adults. You may even be thinking, "I figured it out, and I'm fine now. They will be, too." Except their way of figuring it out, just like their individual needs, may be a different journey they want to feel safe enough to begin with you and your support.

A 504 plan may help them get there. And other stuff they work on with their teachers and counselors. And maybe also exercise, but not just exercise. Your experiences define your identity and belief system. Theirs may be different. If we are able to see many paths to a full rich life, we are less likely to be judgemental of the experience of others, both in our families and in the greater world.

If you want to do things differently as a parent, that means you need to be ready to be uncomfortable. You're going to have to question your beliefs and look for the places in which they are based. Even helpful reasonably accurate beliefs are not universal to everyone we encounter. You're going to have to be ready to take responsibility for those hurts, and you'll have to process the guilt that comes with unintentionally hurting someone. A lot of this work is internal, but you'll likely need to have some tough conversations with people you've hurt, and listen to them with an open heart and a desire to understand other people's experiences of you.

That's all hard work, and it can feel much easier to turn away from that discomfort and go with the flow. Please resist that temptation; your discomfort is very unlikely to kill you. You can feel it even though it might be painful or gross. It's a hard thing that's totally worth it because processing that discomfort and finding a new way forward will benefit you, your kids, and your community in ways you can't imagine.

There are books and podcasts and guided journals out there that can help you process your internalized biases toward yourself and others around you, whether it be judgment of taking meds and requesting a structured 504 plan for testing instead of exercising or judgment of expressing an identity you've never even *heard* of. We've listed some of our favorites at the end of the book, but also suggest you ask people whom you respect for the names of resources they have found most useful.

You may not be able to avoid breathing those toxic fumes, but you can actively work to transform them into fresh air before you breathe them out again. Your kids can breathe that fresher air and be more primed for self-reflection and compassion. If you're choosing to raise them this way even if it's not how you were raised, you're taking a stand and beginning to heal generations of trauma and pain. That's definitely not easy, but it is brave as fuck.

Now's the time to be really compassionate toward yourself and the you that has held the ideas and biases you're examining. The process of learning, growing, and integrating new understandings of yourself and others is ongoing. We don't want to be dishonest about the moments that came before this one—we thought, felt, and experienced those moments, even if they were far from ideal.

And human brains are naturally biased—none of us are ever going to achieve some kind of mythical unbiased perfection. But the idea of learning and growing means that we can own our shit without shame driving the narrative. And when you're mindful of your own trauma, processing, and growth, it's beneficial to the kids you're guiding. It means you're engaging in learning, you're making thoughtful decisions, and you're showing them how to be critically compassionate with themselves as well.

Think about your own experiences of diversity in youth:

- What conversations were in the media in regards to gender, race, and class?

- What are ideas that felt like they were in the bloodstream of your family, church, or school?

- How were the adults who were in charge of the culture then maybe not doing as good a job as you would like to do now when it comes to tough conversations or ideas?

- What do you think you most need to work on? Is it a bias towards yourself or towards those different from you?

- How can you manage your own traumas and fears in ways that are helpful to you while simultaneously guiding a younger person through the process of processing?

# Respect the Identities of Others

Humans are complicated and beautiful creatures. We all have unique experiences and viewpoints and we compile those into our personalities and into the ways we show those personalities to the world. Because we live in a culture that tends to give lip service to "diversity" but in reality, makes people feel shame for their differences, it can get confusing to navigate.

You'll want to create a space where people are valued and respected for who they are. We don't have to agree with all of their choices or opinions; but each one is a human soul (or full of human goo, whatever your understanding), and we owe each other the space to exercise our free will.

Our kids need to know that they are safe to be who they are. That means other people are safe to be themselves too. The identities of others are not up for debate, ridicule, or disdain. In fact, whenever possible, the identities of others should be proactively affirmed by use of appropriate language or actions. Using descriptors (like Black, or tall, or red-headed) can feel complicated to do without sounding like you're putting lots of emphasis on (and likely judging) how a person looks; but using those words is powerfully affirming to people when you do it right.

When everyone is free to be who they are, they also get to define how they want to be talked about, and we have to teach our kids to respect the ways people identify. And we need to talk about the process of reclaiming words, who those words belong to, and how to navigate those conversations. In Bonnie's clinical practice, she works with patients who are working on binge eating patterns or folks who are considering bariatric surgery. If she sees five patients in this area of her practice in one day, she will hear the word "fat" used in five different ways. Some people use it proudly or factually; others speak the word with shame. An adjective/identifier word like that is very personal and is colored by very personal experiences. We owe it to each other to listen, to understand pronouns and identifiers as what they are: personalized definitions of lived experiences. And we don't have to call each other out on using words that may seem pejorative at first.

Turn on your compassion and listen to the experiences of the people who are sharing their identities, and recognize when words are used with pride, or even defiance, versus when they are used in ways that feed self-hatred. A person might say, "I identify as fat because that's a powerful word." Or they might say, "I feel judgmental eyes on me all the time because I am fat and I hate it." Those are very different experiences, and may even come from the same person. It's not our job to define the experiences of others. Our job is to listen, to ask for clarification, and then honor the process another human has gone through to define themselves.

If you get it wrong, for example using incorrect pronouns, acknowledge it but don't make a big deal out of it. A simple, "I'm sorry, I used the wrong pronoun; I'll be more mindful," can go a long way, and is a powerful example for your kids. This applies both to people outside of your family and to your kids as well. If they ask you to use a different name or pronoun, it can be really difficult to change it up because you've got a serious habit of using the old info. Show that you're trying your best to meet their needs and then actually try your best!

How do you want to talk to your family about identities?

- What descriptors do you use for your own identity?

- What about your family and friends?

- Do you feel a mutual respect for your identity and those around you?

- How can you be more affirming of others' identities?

- How will you model how to do repair if there's a misstep?

# Learn from Your Kids

Things change—quickly—and what's acceptable today will be realized as problematic tomorrow. That's progressivism; there's no finish line, and the language and activism are fluid to reflect that reality. If you raise your kids right, they'll learn these things on their own, possibly before you do. So when they correct you, which they inevitably will, how will you respond?

It's our job to accept these corrections and evolutions with grace and openness. The process is not a one-way, top-down distribution of information; it's a feedback loop based in equity and curiosity. We are building the scaffolding, remember? But we are building it so our kids can take over and build it even better.

When this happens, try, "That's an interesting idea and different from what I was taught about this subject. What does this mean to you? Help me understand where it came from so I can learn more about this idea right along with you!"

Or, "When I learned about this a few years ago, we talked about it in another way. I love that some new ideas are coming around on this topic. Tell me more!"

Or, how about, "What are you passionate about on this topic?"

Or even, "I think of this word like 'this,' and it sounds like you think of it like 'that.' Help me understand the differences here. I want to learn more about your understanding of this!" How Gen Alpha defines the word "preppy" is incredibly different from how it was used when Faith and Bonnie were young. Popped collars and alligator logos are not even close to part of the aesthetic.

Because we are all coming from an imperfect background, we can all identify places we wish we'd acted differently, been more (or less) vocal, done more research, or generally just done better. It's possible your kids will have questions about those decision points. If we are to be honest about our growth and learning, it means we have to be welcoming of these call-ins.

Put aside your defensiveness and do some processing of your own shame that comes from being part of the system.

There have been plenty of times when feminism has gotten it wrong and has had a chance to evolve: centering white women, excluding trans women, demonizing sex workers . . . the list is long. It has evolved because people started questioning. When your kids start questioning, are you ready to learn and evolve along with them?

# Have the Tough Conversations

Being a parent is ridiculously hard for eleventy billion reasons. And a good chunk of those reasons have to do with the fact that we are supposed to provide a safe space and calm, measured wisdom to our kids when life goes sideways.

The problem with that is we have no idea what the fuck is going in the world any more than they do, and we definitely don't have all the answers, but our kids are looking to us with the same questions we have. Have you ever had that "oh shit" moment of realizing that you're the adult in the room? And you are looking around for an adultier adult? Like an '80s sitcom parent who is wise and kind and helps everyone feel better about the bad things in life in the space of 22 minutes?

In several states in the United States, it's controversial for teachers (and sometimes even forbidden by law or policy) to even mention race, gender, and sexuality in school, much less teach about them. Libraries are under fire for carrying books about these topics for young people and many are removing those books. The places outside of your family where kids can get accurate information on lots of hot topics are dwindling quickly, which makes it all the more important to have these conversations at home. Especially because you know kids will keep talking to each other about them, and experiencing some of them, and they will be getting perspectives from news and from other adults.

If any of these conversations are particularly loaded in your household, you're not alone. Honestly, same. Bonnie and Faith have homes where these topics are routinely part of the discourse, and they still run into things that make them feel like "What the fuck do I say about this?!"

How the fuck did *we* become the people trying to help our kids navigate a sometimes-awful world? Did we agree to this? Show us where we signed this agreement! Okay, maybe we didn't actually sign a legal document agreeing to be adulty, but at the end of the day, our job as parents is to create a safe place for our children to land and space to figure out who they are and who they want to be in the world. This is no small feat when we're navigating a dumpster fire. There are conversations we have to have with *our* kids that our parents never needed to have with us. We're all operating without a net, trying to figure out how to do the best we can with the tools we've got.

Here are some guidelines that can help keep even the most loaded conversations on the rails.

1. **Assume good will.** When it comes to tough topics and conversations, it's important to go in expecting that your kids are operating from a place of genuine curiosity or desire to understand something new. Assume that they came into contact with some pieces of information that they found confusing and interesting, and they want your take or feedback on it. If it turns out that you have a teenager who is just trying to corner you into a heated debate about political beliefs, you'll still come out of it mostly intact if you go into it with an open heart and mind.

**2. Figure out your own hot buttons.** You know, those topics or ideas that make you sweaty, ragey, nervous, Incredible Hulk-ish? Common ones are everywhere: guns, religion, sexuality, pecan pie is superior to all other pies, Ross and Rachel were on a break . . . you likely know most of the topics that get your heart racing, ready to defend your viewpoint. Or, you may not even realize something *is* a hot button for you until kiddo asks you something and you realize you are totally emotionally activated and are feeling all screamy on the inside. If you know the stuff that gets to you (Faith and Bonnie both have hot-button issues around their advocacy work and the weaponization of religion, for what it's worth), you can feel confident in your ability to discuss it rationally because you've had a chance to think about it. There is some law of physics that ensures that your ouch spots will absolutely be the thing your kids want to talk about most. So figure out the skills you need (like good grounding skills) that will help you turn down the volume on your own reactions so you can be thoughtful and measured with your kiddo(s). It's also okay to own your shit in that regard. Say, "This is an area that I have a lot of strong feelings about. But it's more important to me that you develop your own feelings about it, so I want to be careful to share with you but also hear where you are on the topic." Make space for differences of worldviews. Talk about what you believe as *your* belief system. Talk about who maybe shares it and why others may not. Talk about the fact that your kids, especially as they get older, may not believe everything you believe, and that's a normal and good thing. You want their choices to be conscious and thoughtful, but you don't want them drinking the Flavor Aid from you, their friends, the media, a religious institution, or any other source of beliefs. All these sources of information can have some merit and validity, and who they are in the world may connect to many of them.

3. **Take space if you need to.** Kids are brilliant at swooping in from the sidelines and knocking us off our feet. It's okay to take a moment to figure out what you want to say. It's *not* okay to say "later" and hope the question goes away. Tell your kiddo, "I'm really glad you asked about that. It's cool that you trust me to have this conversation. I need some time to [insert a valid activity—e.g., read more about it, figure out my own thoughts on the topic, finish going to the bathroom for fuck's sake, etc.]. Let's talk about it [insert concrete time—e.g., after dinner this evening when your brother is doing his homework, tomorrow after school, etc.]."

4. **Speak to your child's developmental understanding level.** Younger kids are concrete as pavement and need concrete answers. As they get older, you may expand and discuss more on the philosophy or larger ideas, mindsets, and epistemological differences. Faith learned the hard way to not over academicize conversations with her kids when they were younger. They would nod and tune out because it wasn't at their level of understanding or need. Also, every kid processes in their own way, so you need to know something about your kid and their approach to information to know what level to use for discussion.

5. **Be as open and as calm as possible.** That means you need to make space to focus on the conversation at hand. Use open body language, which may be

something you have to invoke consciously (take a deep breath, roll back your shoulders, drop your crossed arms, lean forward). Set aside your devices and focus on the conversation. Our kids know our body language better than anyone else on the planet. They've brought a topic they were pretty sure was a big one. They are gonna be hyperaware if we are freaking out, and will be less likely to bring us the next big topic. If we can regulate our own nervous system, that will help them regulate theirs and keep the conversation productive.

6. **Reflect back both content and emotions.** Use open ended, non-threatening questions, like "What do you think about [topic]? What have you heard already? What more would you like to know about it?" And speak to emotions, said or unsaid, not just content. Reflect feelings: "Your friend told you they think about hurting themselves. That must be really scary to hear. You're worried about your friend." And then follow up with, "What can I do to support you? I'm here to listen or make a plan or whatever you need."

7. **Don't overthink everything as having a profound, moral-center-developing depth.** Know that some questions/conversations are just that. Don't expect everything to be a bombshell or a revelation or crisis or worst-case scenario.

8. **Know that everything isn't solvable and done within 22 minutes (plus a message from our sponsor).** The solution probably isn't the point; it's the journey and the inquiry. Know that many tough conversations aren't one-shots. They are ongoing, naturally expanding, increasingly complex discussions where we navigate real life and process new information. If the answers

were simple, the conversation would be in a "list of super-easy conversations" zine, but that's not what you're reading! Answer the question you've been asked, and then wait, or say, "Did that answer your question?" or "What other information do you need about this topic?" or "We can talk more about this later after you've thought about it more." Keep the proverbial door open for more exploration.

9. **Keep your eyes, ears, and mind open for chances to have these conversations.** Listen when your young person talks. Ask questions about what they are thinking or what they are experiencing. A lot of needful conversations aren't going to happen because your kid comes up and says, "Hey, I want to talk about community violence because I'm afraid to go to school." Kids quietly worry to themselves on the regular, so part of being the adultiest adult in the room is to find ways to start those conversations ourselves. Look for their hints and openings (there is some immutable law of the universe that says that once kids become teens this will happen when we are busy driving . . . probably something to do with the safety of no eye contact). And if they are silent, jump in anyway. It's okay to talk and not get a response (we promise, they are listening, and they will at some point in the future repeat back the shit you said word for fucking word). Maybe they are silent and mumbly, but it's okay to monologue anyway. You know, like, "I'm sure a lot of people at your school were talking about the most recent school shooting. I'm not sure what they are saying or what you are thinking, but I know how scared I am as your parent and how upset I was to see it on the news. . . ."

10. **Admit that you might be wrong and own it when it happens.** You know what makes us the "woke parenting" experts? Our utter lack of expertise. We are all just hot messes doing the best we can, learning from each other, and learning as we grow. Letting our kids see this process is how we model adulting. We are not as perfectly wise as Elyse and Steven Keaton on *Family Ties* (with a roomful of script writers and editors). We promise that authenticity in parenting creates far more feelings of safety than wrapping ourselves in a cloak of omnipotence and then rushing into every conversation like "Leeeeerrrrrooooooy Jennnnnnnkins!"

## Talk About Race

When Faith's older kid was about eight years old, Faith was driving home and they saw a woman getting arrested in a nearby neighborhood. The police were frisking her and cuffing her against the police car as they were driving by.

Her kid said, "What are they doing?"

Faith responded, "Well, it looks like she's getting arrested."

Her kid was confused, "But she's white, and only Black people get arrested!"

It turns out that Faith's kid had been watching *Law & Order* with grandma and was being flooded with all the stereotypical images of what criminals look like. It was a *huge* wake-up call that these kinds of issues needed to be discussed proactively and repeatedly. She couldn't just model the values that were important to her and hope for the best. She had to be fighting *for* her kids *against* the larger culture.

Families of color in the United States have necessary conversations about race very early in the lives of their children; studies show that white families do not do the same.

White families report that they feel the need to wait for some "safe" or "right" time to talk to their kids about race, racism, and colorism. The right time to talk about racism is immediately. And repeatedly.

Race relations in the United States are fraught and raw, and having real discussions and taking real action is more imperative than ever. We can't shield our children with this "I don't see color" bullshit. In many classrooms in many states across the southern United States, that is the message kids will get because conservative lawmakers have made it difficult-to-illegal to discuss race in any other way, if at all. But we don't have to stick to that message. If DEI programs are losing funding, it falls on us even more than before. The work of dismantling racism belongs to all of us, of course, but white families must own more of the work than they have in the past. To be silent, to stand aside, to decline to participate—it is unacceptable. The time for action is now, and your feminist, intersectional, woke, DEI, and CRT-lovin' family is the place to start.

Race is a topic that is all-encompassing to American life. It always has been, but for modern parents, especially those of us who are white or white-passing, it has been even more front and center over the past decade. The protests in the summer of 2020 were another very visible example of the need to proactively discuss race in our homes and to actively make changes in our relationships and communities.

In the summer of 2020, Bonnie's daughter was six. She saw the protests on TV and started asking questions about what she saw. Bonnie's had a lot of tough conversations with her kid over the years, but talking about the police brutality of 2020 was something else altogether. Bonnie and her kid both felt the gravity and urgency of the conversation, but Bonnie moved through it as slowly and thoughtfully as she could. The conversation that specific day ended with them talking about the parents of the people who were killed that summer and how much they must miss their kids who were taken too soon. And then they checked out some books about the history of civil rights and they made donations to social justice organizations in their community. The conversation is important, but it isn't enough. We can show our kids that we learn, we grow, and then we show up, in all the ways we can, to do the work. And we continue to engage with these tough topics. One conversation and a few well-meaning donations don't get the job done or let us off the hook, but we also can't pass up chances to do those things.

These conversations may mean we have to wrestle with some defensive or uncomfortable feelings around our privilege, our lack of knowledge/understanding of history, or that we are descendants of people who were involved in the institution of slavery. We are not the decisions our ancestors made; we can choose to be accountable to the history of slavery and systemic racism by actively working against it. Even if your family owned a plantation, you can choose love and activism, and you can own the fact that slavery was monstrous. You didn't have a plantation, but likely benefited from a system that allowed your family to have one. And that's important to recognize so we can *fix broken shit.* We haven't met anyone demanding that people apologize for the actions of their ancestors, but what we are demanding is necessary societal change. The legacy of slavery lives in white supremacy; how do your actions push back against or perpetuate this system of violence?

The general discussions you're engaging in with your family, about power and safety and allyship, lead many families into discussions specifically about race and systemic racial inequalities. Don't think it's done or that they get it. We never know when a *Law & Order*–esque counter-message has infiltrated their subconscious and is informing their view of the world.

As parents, we know that each time we tell our child goodbye at school drop-off or as they walk out the front door with friends, it could be the last time. None of us are guaranteed safety in this life, and understanding mortality is among the higher-stress truths of parenthood. But, if you are the parent of a white (or "passing") child, understand that your child will be given the benefit of the doubt in situations that children of color will not. A white child is less likely to be harassed or killed by police, is less likely to be arrested for a minor crime, and is more likely to come home to you safely. Understand this, and then dive into the work that needs to be done to help all our kids be safer.

One of the ongoing effects of white supremacy is colorism and passing. People with lighter skin are often viewed more favorably than people with darker skin, and that's just straight-up systemic racism showing up in another place in our lives. Faith and her kids are mixed, but have enough pass privilege to have a different experience of the world than someone more melanated. One of the assorted kiddos in her extended family is much darker than the rest, even though most everyone is multiracial. And some racist/colorist bullshit occurred on one side of the family, which became *yet another fucking growth opportunity* within the entire family. And praise be to every momma bear involved for being loud and insistent that this wasn't an "apologize and move on" situation.

Bonnie has been doing some deep emotional work with several clients who are coming to terms with the effects of colorism in their own families. They've seen and experienced that other family members get better treatment if they have lighter skin, and that's hurtful. Because white supremacy operates in a hierarchy of power (where the power comes from being pale

147

af), all the degrees of whiteness or paleness come with degrees of power within the system. It really sucks to see that play out in our own experiences and within our own families where we want to be loved and accepted wholly.

Doing antiracism work is far from easy, but it is imperative to do it anyway. It can take a real toll on your mental and spiritual health. Building up your self-care routine, and showing this to your kids, is an important part of keeping up the pace. So often, we feel real physical pain when we read the news or engage in racial work; we have to take time to replenish and come back to the work with newfound tenacity every single time.

Obviously, this could be a whole book in and of itself. This book is an overview of a lot of different shit, not an in-depth analysis of anything in particular. So with this topic, *especially* this topic, please seek out writing and ideas from people of color. Look for workshops and gatherings in your area that center on race and racism. Do the work of unpacking white privilege yourself with other activists and scholars. Look for and fight against racism in the institutions that have shaped your life. Share the background and additional information you learn with your children. Encourage your children to talk about their experiences with race and racism, and help them navigate this complicated landscape with empathy and courage.

- What are your experiences with white supremacy and colorism in your family or life?

- Are you carrying any of those internalized biases that may be affecting you or your family?

- How often do you have people in your home, around your table, that don't look like you and the other members of your family?

- What types of media do you consume that reflect the complexity of different cultures rather than stereotypes?

- What comments, stories, presumptions have you heard made about you and our family? What about other people and their families that don't look like you?

- What kinds of things have you seen or heard that made you uncomfortable in that regard? Would you like help coming up with responses for the future?

## Talk About Gender

Gender has nothing to do with who you have sex with, what sexual organs you were born with, or how you present on the outside. Sometimes we express ourselves through those means, but gender is more complex and way more of an internal state of being than you may have realized. Gender is the way we experience life along (and outside) the spectrum of masculinity and femininity, and these experiences are diverse and impacted by many factors, including our culture, our religion, our family of origin, and our own feelings about our gender.

Gender exists along a continuum of experiences and can be very fluid for some people and very rigid for others. This may vary based on age, where someone lives, and the overall culture a person lives within.

SUPPORT YOUR KID IN THEIR EXPERIENCE OF GENDER

Kids get a lot of messages about gender and gender roles. And just as adults experience gender differently at different times in our lives or different spheres, kids experience this fluidity as well. As they grow, you may notice them experimenting with the ways they express gender (think clothing, hairstyles, name, or pronouns) and that can be jarring for some parents. In her office, Bonnie coaches parents to relax when they are nervous about this; hairstyles and pronouns aren't permanent, and it's okay for kids to play around with them. No harm done. For parents who are nervous about this exploration, the impermanence gives them space to let the process happen. When it's time to discuss and pursue more permanent transition options, these parents feel less resistant because they've had time to adjust.

If your child is consistent, persistent, and insistent that they are a different gender than the one assigned to them at birth, it may be more than exploration. As more visibility and support is accessible for people in the trans community, it's becoming more common for young people to identify openly as trans. Support your child by being open and listening to their feelings. Many trans and gender nonconforming (GNC) adults can tell you about how they knew their truths very early in their lives, but not everyone knows from a young age, so this may happen at any time—even after they've moved out and are on their own. A safe and affirming home and school experience is invaluable as people are defining their gender experiences.

As visibility has increased, so also has the pushback from conservatives. A real moral panic has swept through the United States, and it deeply affects trans folks, their families, and people who support them. A concerted effort exists online for anyone who works for trans rights (especially for youth trans rights) to be called a groomer or a pedo and then to be threatened with doxxing or physical violence. Lots of misinformation and propaganda surrounds the discussions of gender-affirming care (for example, the idea that minors are being forced into surgeries), and those lies fan the flames.

For example, the idea of "Rapid Onset Gender Dysphoria" began appearing in the mid-2010s. Though the original study was found to be limited and flawed, and ROGD isn't in any way an accepted clinical diagnosis, the term began to gain traction among anti-LGBTQ+ crusaders and politicians. The study and term have since been cited in hundreds of bills across the country that block or limit access to gender-affirming care. The effects of this made-up term are incredibly real; in Texas, for example, parents, guardians, and care providers (doctors, therapists, etc.) can be investigated by Child Protective Services for validating a non-cis child's gender identity. It can be challenging to know how to support your child's exploration of gender identity in that culture.

If your child is very into exploring their gender identity or expression, a good starting point is to find support for yourself in an online community like PFLAG or your local LGBTQ+ groups. Most larger communities have peer-led groups and family outing activities you can check out. Bonnie and Faith live in the deep and scary South but have both served on (different!) boards that provide these types of services. Additionally, there may be resources at your child's school; lots of schools have gay-straight alliance groups (GSAs)—or, more and more commonly, queer-straight alliance groups (QSAs)—that work to create inclusive school spaces. Leverage the resources around you and see where there may be holes in the support network.

You may want to create a team of gender-affirming professionals to support your family in the process. Bonnie has had a lot of trans teens on her caseload over the years, and therapy sessions are generally spent talking about hopes, fears, challenges, and questions about what it means to be trans or deciding to transition either socially or medically, along with the general stressors that all teens face, regardless of gender expression. She also has worked with several parents of teens who are trans. Those sessions give space to parents who are scared their child may be discriminated against or be otherwise unsafe, have questions about the transition process, or are even processing the grief that can accompany big changes in life. Your family deserves support and an affirming space to process the big feelings that come with shifting identities.

Families of trans kids face specific types of stressors. They have to be ready to advocate for safe spaces in school (getting teachers and administrators to use correct pronouns and names, allowing kids to use the restroom of their gender, or managing bullying). There may be transphobia within the family's social circle or extended family members (like grandparents, family friends, or church).

Conservative state legislatures have very purposefully targeted trans youth with nasty bills that limit their ability to seek gender-affirming care, that prohibit them from participating in sports, or that enforce bathroom/locker room use to "birth gender." These examples of systemic transphobia can be devastating to trans youth and their families and are a unique stressor in their daily lives. If your child is trans (or even suspected of being trans in some states), you're going to need a strong support system to help you manage the discrimination and aggressions your family may face. With Texas weaponizing Child Protective Services against the families and care providers of trans youth, several programs banded together, including the ACLU, to help us navigate these times. If you are in a similar situation, there are lawyers donating their time to the cause, and you can request preemptive support of your family plus training for your children on how to respond (politely but firmly insistent on having their parent present) if they are questioned by any state officials about their gender.

Bonnie also has a few clients who come from families who are not affirming, supportive, or interested in their gender. If your child is trans or interested in exploring their gender, and you find you're struggling to engage on the topic, please at least find them a safe adult they can talk about it with. Trans youth whose families are not affirming are much more likely to die by suicide than other teens. Gender is powerful in our lives, and if parents cannot affirm and support trans kids, the rejection is felt deeply. You will have your own feelings about your child's gender, and that's valid, but your child needs someone safe to talk to while you process.

Separate therapy, then family therapy, support groups, etc., cannot be under-suggested by us if this is the case. Faith has done both individual sessions and group classes for anxious family members of gender-diverse kids and cannot understate how helpful it is to get out all your fears and worries and concerns with someone that isn't your kid and won't take your fears personally. Your willingness to be open to information may be of enormous benefit to aforementioned kid, no matter what path your family ultimately choses.

There are also lots of good resources online about social transition and medical transition options, (including puberty blockers, hormones, and surgery). This can help you figure out your comfort level and starting point for helping your child bloom into who they are. If you are fearful that it is an impulse, not their true identity, there is tons of information around exploring social transition without making any more complex (and sometimes permanent) changes. Faith just sent the Human Rights Commission article on coming out as trans at work to a young client who was anxious about that process at their new job. If you aren't sure where to start, your local LGBTQ+ resource center will likely have some great resources for you.

Okay, so, how do you want to start to talk about gender in your family? You might have practice, "What if . . ." conversations, like, "What if your friend tells you they are trans? Like, he's spending the night at the house, and y'all are playing video games, and he says, 'Oh by the way, I was born with a vagina'?" Let your kid think out loud about the ways they can support their friends. What is their own experience of gender and what do they see in their social groups or classes? What do they want to know and what do they need to know? What might make their friend feel comfortable versus uncomfortable in the process? Help them troubleshoot problematic relationships, and show that you support them in forming their own ideas and approaches. Help them recognize and remove themselves from dangerous people and situations.

It can feel difficult and overwhelming to provide guidance when the terminology around gender and gender expression is expanding so quickly. It's okay to say, "I don't really know what that term means, let's look it up!" Faith and Bonnie have done training on the topic and have been presented with a question in which they had to do just that.

This expansion is a reflection of society catching up with the complexity of human experience, and we can share that with our kids. Point out that language changes to reflect how society changes and that is exactly what is happening, so if someone is using neopronouns (a third-person pronoun that don't express a particular gender), it's because that suits them best . . . and we can respect that person by using that pronoun.

Once you feel more confident about the terminology, you can be more respectful in navigating conversations, questions, and ideas around gender as a whole. Most people will experiment in some ways with their gender identity and presentation. Allowing a respectful space for your kids to explore their identities and ask questions will be very valuable as they navigate relationships with themselves and others. As with everything else, you are going to be listening for toxic cultural messages and offering them chances to challenge them. Here are some starting points around gender identity, and we will offer more on how we ascribe gendered attributes to every damn thing in the next section.

Other conversations you may have with younger kiddos will be based on what they see and have questions about. For example, pronouns: "Pronouns are a way of recognizing someone's gender identity. Most people who use the pronouns she/her/hers, for example, identify as a girl or woman. So when you see that, that's what they are telling you about themself. What are your pronouns? Mine are she/her/hers. I decided that because it's what feels best for me."

Or, what does it mean to not be cisgender at all? "When people are born, the doctor looks at them and decides based on whether they have a penis or a vulva if they are a boy or a girl. This is called being assigned male at birth (if you have a penis) or assigned female at birth (if you have a vulva). As we get older, sometimes our brain tells us that's wrong, and our brain knows we are actually not a boy or a girl but the opposite, or someone in between, or someone else altogether. And that is where the term transgender comes from. Trans just means 'across' from what you were assigned at birth. And nonbinary means you don't fit in one category or another."

As your kiddos get older, they may have more specific questions. You may be able to answer these questions for them, or you may be able to find them age-appropriate materials to help them understand. For example, *I Am Jazz* is a great book for younger children, while *Being Jazz: My Life As a*

*(Transgender) Teen* is more appropriate for older kids. Both are about Jazz Jennings's experience as a young girl who happens to be transgender.

Your kids may have questions and concerns about that, and you can be both honest and comforting to them, saying something like, "It is pretty scary right now, but there are lots of people working hard to protect kids. There are a bunch of groups and lawyers fighting to protect the parents and doctors and therapists that are working to help kids get the medical care they need. So if you have any friends that are worried or you have something you want to talk to us about, we will find ways to help and protect you or anyone else who needs help and protection. Not all adults are safe, but a lot of them are. We will always help you find the ones that are, and we will also work very hard to be the ones that are."

Prepare yourself for these conversations by sorting out some of your own thoughts and feelings by considering the following:

- How do you define gender?

- What messages have you gotten about gender, gender expression, or gender roles, and how does this play out in your life?

- How do you define and experience your own gender?

- How do you communicate that definition to other people in your life?

- How do you express your felt sense of gender in various areas of life?

- How do you see gender expression happening for your child or their friends?

- How do you want to talk about gender with your kids?

Gender identity and expression aside? Let's talk about gender coding. Part of keeping everyone in an immutable gender binary means creating rules for what is allowed if you are "boy" or "girl." And definitely no in-between. A kiddo who is as cisgender as Faith and Bonnie may be confused about how they perform gender in their daily lives. And life is already difficult enough to have to worry about that shit.

Basic rule here, alright? There are no "boy things" or "girl things," okay? There are just "toys" or "clothes" or whatever. Boys can like what they want. Girls can like what they want. People can like what they want. That rule will help you with so many gender ideas and questions. It gives you permission to give kids of all ages the space to experiment with gender. To have freedom to find the activities, toys, clothes, and *lives* that spark their interests and give them joy. Get your gendered ideas out of here right now, and start by being aware of the moment when all the messages that you grew up with start sprouting up like weeds in your conversations.

Occasionally, Bonnie's daughter would ask, "Is that a boy or a girl?" about a character in a book or movie. Bonnie always answered with, "What do you think?" and her daughter usually said something like, "I don't know; maybe it's just a cow?" Like, on further inspection, maybe it doesn't matter.

Maybe the Shy Little Kitten is a girl when you read the story on Tuesday and a boy when you read it on Wednesday. Point out astronauts that are women and men that are teachers. Lean into your discomfort with ambiguous or flexible gender, and see how it feels to be more open. Let that flexibility guide you into bigger areas, like toys, clothes, and careers. Don't limit your kid's imagination or potential by creating boxes full of gendered stuff and then forcing your kid into those boxes.

If your kids have questions about gender and gender nonconforming behavior, talk about how that's changed over time. Show them old pictures online, and point out that women used to always wear dresses because that's what they were supposed to do. And now we know how silly that is because sometimes women wear jeans because they like them better and think they're more comfortable. And sometimes boys wear dresses, because they like them better and think they're more comfortable.

And there are all kinds of ways gender can present throughout our lifetimes. While Faith's son is pretty cishet manly (he's pretty much an epic bro, and Bonnie can attest to that), he does like to experiment with scents and will sometimes wear her perfume with his suit and tie. He finds it hilarious when women ask him, "Dude . . . is that Chanel No. 5?"

Here are some ideas that might get the conversation going with elementary-age kiddos:

- "It bothers me to hear you describe specific types of clothing as 'only for boys.' What does that mean to you?"

- "Lots of people wear makeup or nail polish because it's fun! I'm sorry you have heard the idea that it's only for girls. Would you like to paint your nails and see how you like it?"

With older kids:

- "Now that you're older, have you noticed that certain things most people like to do are considered weird based on whether you're a boy or a girl?"

- "Are there things you wish you could do/enjoy that you are afraid you might get teased about because it's a girl thing or a boy thing?"

## Talk About Sexuality

Sexuality is a different conversation than gender, though they often happen together or in related ways. Gender is how we feel about and express our male/female/nonbinary-ness; sexuality is who we are (or aren't) attracted to romantically or sexually. Just like gender, though, sexuality is a spectrum and can vary over the course of a lifetime.

One key piece of advice is to avoid making assumptions about who our kids may or may not be attracted to later in life. Don't make assumptions that they want to get married at all, or that they will marry or date people of "opposite" sex or gender. A lot of Bonnie's clients are adolescents, and almost all of them have a story about one of their parents saying something like, "I don't really care who you date as long as they aren't jerks," and Bonnie really likes this approach. The important parts of dating, sex, and sexuality are the ways we find safety, challenges, and excitement in other people. Encouraging young people in your life to look for the safe and fun people is the key takeaway.

Some people aren't sexually attracted to other people at all; they may or may not enjoy romantic relationships—both of which are also valid ways of being human. It's important to share that a person isn't broken if their sexual and/or romantic orientation is, (D) none of the above, because they may not hear or see that from anyone else.

Our kids will need support in feeling safe to explore their sexuality and sexual/romantic identities. They need to know that if they are LGBTQ+, they have adults in their lives who will hold a safe space for letting them figure out how that fits into their overall identity and approach to the world. If they use labels or terminology you're unfamiliar with, please feel free to gently ask what those terms mean to the young person you're talking to. Bonnie has a client who ended up making a PowerPoint presentation when they wanted to come out to their parents as pansexual. They were pretty sure their parents wouldn't know the terminology, and they didn't want the conversation to get derailed by definitions. Keep an open mind and open ears when a young person is letting you into a sensitive part of their psyche and identity.

"Coming out" will look different for everyone and is a process, not a singular event. We hope for a day when people don't have to be scared to come out—or maybe they don't have to come out at all—because the world is accepting and there is not a presumed "normal" way to be that we have to announce we don't ascribe to, and people are far less nosy about who we want to love. But for right now, LGBTQ+ peeps need a safe place to have this conversation, a place where they are affirmed and loved and held as precious. Remember, too, that coming out belongs to the person coming out! If they've trusted you, it doesn't mean you go and tell other people about it. Just because they are okay with you knowing doesn't mean they are ready for other people in their life to know; that may even include other parents or family members.

Make sure you're a person who supports LGBTQ+ youth to come out in their own time, with their own plans, and in the order they choose. And, alternately, if they specifically ask you to tell people, or address issues with other adults that they are facing (you know, misgendering them, telling them that they are just having a "phase," and other crappy behavior), then you absolutely should. This is allyship as a verb, right? Giving them authority over how they share their identity, while standing by their side in bodyguard mode is one of the best gifts you can give your kiddo. And it's fuckin' free.

The sexuality conversations you're having with young people in your life will encompass more than coming out, obviously. Being ready to talk about consent, risk-reduction strategies, and other logistics will be helpful—and we'll give you some tools for talking about sex and consent in another chapter. But we think of this conversation more generally as guidance into the sometimes-fraught world of romance, courting, and being respectful of potential partners. The logistics are there, obviously, but this can also be a conversation about all the joy and fun that comes from meeting new people, feeling curious and excited, and learning new things about ourselves by being in these types of relationships.

## Talk About Religion and Spirituality

Almost all humans have some kind of connection with the world outside ourselves. We may express that through religion, spirituality, or some form of secular humanism. And these topics are just as important as any others, even if we don't have some kind of formal religious practice and are not raising our kids with same-said practice.

Faith's parents, while devout Catholics, were also devoutly progressive. There were a lot of conversations about what they loved about the church, what they found challenging, and how their beliefs sat in the discomfort of hoping for change. They also encouraged her to have something bigger than herself. It didn't have to be Catholicism, but it should be something. They encouraged her to attend other churches and discuss what she liked and didn't like. It was pretty amazing to be able to be horrified by a sermon at a friend's church and go home and process that experience with a parent.

And like everything else, we want to give our children a space to grow and to think, right? The way Faith now expresses that "something bigger than oneself" has evolved into more of a sense of wonder about the world.

We can express religion or spirituality or some form of secular humanity by rote. Without any real engagement with something bigger. Or we can experience life, in its vast array, with a sense of *wonder*. That is where our sense of purposeful belonging resides. When our belief system, our ritual, our engagement in the process serves to care for people and include them rather than judge and exclude them. As long as that's our operating system, we are aiming for good humaning.[5]

Another piece of this conversation revolves around helping your kid navigate other peoples' religious or spiritual beliefs. Bonnie is not religious, but many people in her life are. She talks to her daughter about how everyone finds their own connection to the world and to other people, and some of us find that in religion. Some of us find it in art and music, or quiet parks, or volunteering, or any other myriad ways. As long as someone is not using their religious beliefs to oppress another, we can respect each other and be curious about other approaches to the spiritual. Deep and meaningful conversations happen in that curious and mystical space.

Leaving religion and spirituality open to discussion may mean that your kid chooses a really different belief system than the one you possess. Spiritual experiences are deep and personal; it might feel emotionally fraught to have these conversations with your kid when they choose a different path than the one you're on.

Consider the following:

---

5 Faith was really inspired in this belief by an episode of the podcast *On Being*, in which Nikki Giovanni asked Dr. Mary Catherine Bateson about the difference between religion and spirituality. Dr. Bateson was the daughter of Margaret Mead and Gregory Bateson, avowed atheists, while she became Episcopalian.

- How will you handle a kid who is atheist while you're deeply connected to God?

- What if they are leaning toward a more conservative type of worship system and you're not comfortable with that?

- What space does spirituality or religion hold in your home?

- Is there room for different viewpoints and experiences?

- What messages do you want your kids to hear from you regarding religion and spirituality?

- What beliefs about this are you carrying from childhood?

## Talk About Disability and Accessibility

Here's a thing we can maybe all agree on: we all have a body. And those bodies are diverse and wonderful and strong in many different ways. Kids naturally notice diversity and are generally curious. That leads them to ask questions when they see people using wheelchairs or people who are accompanied by service animals. As parents, we want to encourage their curiosity about all the ways bodies can work or move, but we can sometimes feel uncomfortable in the moment when our kid is pointing or asking loud questions in a grocery store.

However, to ignore diversity of physical abilities is to ignore the people living in diverse bodies, and we don't want that. So, start early in talking to your kids about how people exist with differing physical abilities and nonvisible differences that may be physical or neurological. Provide them with books, toys, movies and other media that are inclusive of people who think or move in different or assisted ways. Help kids (and other adults) to reframe our ideas of accessibility; a wheelchair, for example, is not a restriction. It's a tool that's available to help people move and live. Societal limits on accessibility are where we can focus our activism and support of people who use wheelchairs. Creating an inclusive society means we make space in our own lives for diversity.

In recent years, parents have gotten really good at asking each other about food allergies. We all became very mindful that a few parents have kids who have serious reactions to peanuts and we started asking about food allergies when we planned birthday parties or neighborhood gatherings. Then we started just saying it when we invited people like, "Come over for Aiden's seventh birthday party! We will have nut-free snacks and drinks. See you soon!" And then that started to translate to adult companions also; asking a friend to dinner started to sound like, "Hey, wanna hang out and eat some food? What do you feel like, or do you have anything you're not eating right now?"

We can normalize this type of planning around physical limits too, and make it totally normal and inclusive. "Come over to the park for Aiden's seventh birthday party! We will have nut-free snacks and drinks. And the park has wheelchair ramps and bathrooms with diaper changing stations. Let me know if there are other things y'all need. See you soon!"

If you're able-bodied, do your research about what's available in your community or where you can add your voice to advocacy work. If you're able-bodied and raising a kid who is disabled and you want society to do right by them, finding local advocacy resources will help you not have to fight that fight alone. If you're living with your own disability, it doesn't disappear when you live in parentland . . . having your own friends who joyfully make inclusive space is vital.

It's also important to create space for people with invisible disabilities. Autistic people and those with sensory processing disorders or other types of neurodivergence may need different accommodations as well. The important thing is to be mindful of physical diversity and neurodiversity in the world and to make space everywhere you can. This willingness can also be included in the invite to Aiden's seventh birthday party. Something like, "This will likely be a typical loud and chaotic event for a seven-year-old, so please don't hesitate to reach out if your kiddo needs any accommodations to attend without being overwhelmed."

Faith's kids both had friends (some are very dear friends) with mobility needs, neurodiversity diagnoses, etc. We've always figured out accommodations that worked, and it was never a huge deal (e.g., when she was driving one of her son's best buds, he would switch to his foldable wheelchair that could fit in her car). Faith has needed mobility support most of her life, and while she hasn't had to use crutches or the like in some time (*knocks wood*), she notices accessibility everywhere she goes. And if you haven't needed to, you may not. And it may feel overwhelming to think, "This too?" but like a peanut allergy, it becomes another thing we learn to pay attention to. And it makes us more inclusive people *and* is good for our neuroplasticity.

If you're gearing up to be the person in your friend group (or your kid's friend group) that advocates for inclusivity and accessibility, be ready for it to maybe get complicated. That's part of the fun, honestly, like a logic puzzle. How will you handle it when one kid has severe animal dander allergies and another needs to bring their service dog to the BBQ? What about the kid who's a loud talker getting paired with someone with a sound-sensitivity?

Here's a chance to use your thoughtfulness and creativity; the limitations of a plan or a space are just a problem to be solved. Ask what people need to be comfy, and start brainstorming from there. San Antonio has an amusement park that's been specifically designed to be accessible to all people; it's a cool place to visit and see some of the ways accessibility issues can be addressed to make a space fun for everyone. Bonnie and Faith can't wait to hear about your beautiful and flexible plans for Aiden's next birthday party.

## Talk About Mental Health

Back in the chapter about your self-care and health, we talked about how to assess your own mental health needs and how to advocate for the treatment plan you need to feel your best. It is incredibly likely that your kid will need this type of care as well, especially since mental health and safety is a large and all-encompassing topic that you'll probably need to keep open in family conversations throughout your lives. Mental health is routinely listed among the top concerns parents have for their kids, and rightfully so. There's a lot of awareness around mental health care and a concerted effort to make it easier to access and for it to carry less stigma. Life is hard for our kids, and they need us to hand them the mental health tools to help them cope.

Like most topics in this book, discussions around mental health are ongoing, and it's always a good time to start having them in age-appropriate ways. For little kids, focus conversations on managing big moods, safe ways to deal with feelings, self-soothing, and processing verbally or physically when we need to. Older kids may need discussions about bullying, self-worth, asking for help from trusted people, or managing stress or perfectionism. Kids in the age range of 8–14 are particularly vulnerable to the stress of mental health and the drop of self-confidence that comes with the onset of puberty. Teens and youth might need support in processing their own mental health struggles, or supporting their friends, or dealing with the big emotions that come with life transitions.

Many teens, if they are not themselves experiencing struggles with nonsuicidal self injury, depression, anxiety, or suicidal thoughts, have friends who are experiencing all of that and more. So your guidance here might be for your own kiddo, and it might also be for supporting your kiddo while they support their friends. You'll have to know the difference between when to provide supportive listening and guidance and when to intervene, contact other parents, or implement other safety measures.

Your own experiences of mental health struggles and support are welcome in this conversation as long as you're sharing appropriately. It's totally okay for your kids to know that you take meds and/or go to therapy. Talking openly about caring for your mental health and how you address it gives kids permission to talk to you openly about their inner worlds and experiences.

Some kids will go to therapy to process stress or big feelings. Some will need support for trauma or family struggles. Some will go because their parents are therapists and we make them. Kids, like adults, can learn to come and go from therapy as needed, as long as their needs are met and they feel stable. Treatment plans for young people can be very flexible when only therapy is involved. If kiddos need meds or specialized treatments, the plans may be less flexible, but they're still meant to support the kid and the family as much as possible.

If you are thinking that maybe your kiddo could benefit from a specific diagnosis, mental health support is available for that as well. Diagnosis can be a double-edged sword: On the one hand, the diagnosis can be helpful for accessing treatment, medications and accommodations. But on the other, sometimes insurance companies or jobs can hold a diagnosis like that against a person; while this is definitely unfair, it is a consideration in the overall ethics of diagnosis.

Weigh the pros and cons of seeking an official diagnosis for neurodivergence (autism, ADHD, or anxiety disorders like obsessive compulsive disorder). Obviously, these can significantly affect the way a person moves in the world, and if a diagnosis is necessary for accommodations at work or school, it's likely worth the effort. If the diagnosis isn't a requirement, we don't think people need to necessarily invest the time/money into getting an official assessment. We're okay with clients telling us they suspect something like ADHD and we are okay with clients using words that fit their experiences. It's also okay with us if clients want to eschew labels altogether and instead want to focus on managing the impact of symptoms.

Major depression and anxiety are widespread mental health issues for young people, and it can be difficult to find the right support for them. Talk therapy and support groups can be effective. Sometimes medications can also be helpful, but meds are not typically tested in adolescent populations, so some providers are reluctant to prescribe. Watching your kid struggle with these conditions is hard and often scary.

What if you learn or believe that your child is suicidal? In the United States, the national suicide hotline is available in English and Spanish, and you can reach it by calling or texting 988. That will connect you with resources near you so you can get the support you need to guide your family through the scary times. Additionally, there are hotlines that specialize in specific populations, like LGBTQ+ youth, rape and incest survivors, and teens.

Faith and Bonnie, as clinicians, want to give you a heads up that if your kiddo has a mental health crisis, they will likely need ongoing support. We've both had experiences working with families that jumped right in when issues were acute but struggled to understand that their kid was telling them they still really benefited from the therapy, meds, and other treatments even though they were no longer actively suicidal.

Parents are often so relieved that we moved past the immediate danger part, that they sometimes read that as meaning their kiddos are now "better." Bless Gen Z and our upcoming Gen Alphas for recognizing that mental health care is no different from physical health care, we encourage you to have ongoing conversations and ongoing support in getting appropriate treatment.

# SAFE(ER)

*F*aith and Bonnie have invested in a lot of bubble wrap over the years. But despite doing so, they have not been able to protect their kids from the hurtful things that happen in the world around them. There's not enough bubble wrap in the world, they've found. Also, their kids don't want to wear it to school because it's apparently "uncool" to wear bubble wrap as outerwear.

You get it.

"Bad things happening" is high on the list of things people asked for help in discussing with their kids. Death, divorce, illness, war, violence, hate crimes, pandemic, bullying, car crashes, tripping and falling, tooth decay, never feeling fulfilled . . . the list of threats to our kids' safety can feel really long, and of course, the media blows some of the dangers out of proportion while others can feel almost taboo to talk about. And there are no prepackaged answers to all of their questions or to our fears. Talking about harm and safety requires being honest. About facts and our feelings. About what we can control and what we cannot. It requires showing them, through our actions, how we try to make good choices every day to stay safe without being limited by fear.

A sense of proportion is key when it comes to figuring out what safety concerns to focus on. Bonnie's husband has a funny saying: he never learned how to fight a shark, therefore never wants to go to the beach. Faith and Bonnie found this a funny comment, but it got them thinking about the things we teach our kids about being safe in the world and the far more important things we leave out.

We grew up in the era of "stranger danger," but no one told us that the people who might hurt us the most are those closest to us. Imagine if those of us who are now adults had been encouraged to speak out if we had ever been uncomfortable with or harmed by other family members, neighbors, pastors, teachers, etc.?

We keep warning our kids about sharks but not about the possible pedophiles in our families. While sharks do swim in the deep waters, jellyfish will come right up on the shore and are much harder to spot. The Bermuda Triangle and quicksand ended up not posing any threats to us, but the day-to-day people in our lives . . . ? Talk to your kids about the real dangers that can exist close to home, and help them build their defenses. Which doesn't mean that sharks shouldn't be feared, but they may not be the most likely threat.

# Protect Your Kid from Bullies

Most adults know what it's like to face a bully. That dickhead in traffic cutting you off and then yelling at you. The shitty boss who undermines and gaslights you. The online trolls who threaten to burn your house down because you shared a list of reasons Texas is the best state (it's not, we know it's not, don't doxx us, kthnx).

Imagine how much harder those types of interactions are for a kid (or maybe you don't have to imagine because you remember your own experiences); feeling small and even more helpless in the face of a ragey and mean person, who is probably not a stranger, but is in fact the person who sits behind you in math class. We have to coach our kids in the ways they can stand up to bullies while keeping themselves as safe as possible, and while keeping their own moral compasses intact.

So, first, what is bullying? Essentially, it is a *repetitive, intentional hurting* of a person by another person or group. That hurting can be physical, emotional, reputation-focused, and isolating. It can happen in person or through digital means like social media or phones. The person experiencing the bullying will typically have a difficult or impossible time putting a stop to the unwanted behavior. When we are teaching kids how to identify bullying, it may take some focused conversation to hear what is true in the lives of young people right now. They get to decide what treatment feels okay and what doesn't, and we can support them in speaking up against anything that's over the line.

Start by coaching them in some basic ideas like safety in numbers. Studies show that if a large number of people in a group speak out against bullying, it's harder for a bully to find a specific target, and they may even face social repercussions for trying. This means that when our kids see a bullying situation, it's important for them to speak up. They need to try and stay calm and use a powerful voice and body stance as they come into the interaction, and they need to do this in a public place. They can use humor to redirect the conversation or distract the focus of the bully. They can use a calm voice, look the bully in the eye, and use clear language like, "Stop this. No one likes it." Let your kid practice with you, have them recite some of the things they'd want to say to the bully to make sure they are clear, concise, and calm.

Some schools of thought recommend documenting the bullying your child is experiencing or witnessing, because that list of transgressions can motivate them to action or back them up with an authority figure if they get in trouble for standing up to the bully. Your kid needs to know that they might need to use physical defenses, but they should use them as a last resort. Hopefully, the correct intervention would happen before any bullying crossed that line, but it's important for them to be prepared. And discuss the possible consequences of becoming physical at school and other places they may be. Tell them what *your* expectations of them are. That is, if they defend themselves appropriately, are you going to advocate for them at school, even when they are then suspended for doing so?

Also, note that most of the information about bullying focuses on children bullying other children. Not adults bullying children. And not just the weirdo adults in line next to them at Family Dollar, but adults that have a level of power over their lives. The family member, teacher, pastor, or parent of a friend. Encourage them to tell you about everyone who contributes to them feeling like shit so you can help them parse out if there is a problematic adult in their life. If your kids are going about their lives, following your rules, and another adult has a problem with them? You want your kids to tell you and also politely tell the person in question to take it up with you and back off of them.

And teach them how to communicate in ways that won't get them in more trouble. Faith always told her kids to be the polite one and let her do the heavier stuff, which, come to think of it, was the same advice she gave her clients when she was a court liaison case manager. This changes the power differential, and the bullying adult in question will learn to either pick on someone their own size or shut their piehole.

Faith's son was pretty boss when he told a school administrator, "I'll turn my shirt inside out for the rest of the day because you feel it is inappropriate. However, my mom bought me this shirt and we both like it, and I don't know that either of us would agree that it was in violation of the school dress code. Could you please call her to discuss your concerns?"

You can also start coaching them to politely question as they get older. Saying to the meddling aunt, for example, "I'm not sure why you are commenting on my weight in a negative way. It feels unkind, is that your intent? I thought we were here for a birthday party, which is supposed to be a fun event." And the crap "jokes" people tell as a subtle form of bullying? A response that almost always works is, "I don't get it, why is that funny?" It puts the onus back on the adult in question to explain themselves.

Finally, just let your kids know that you support them no matter what, and that standing up to a bully is an important part of your family culture of fostering kindness and respect in the world. We will raise children who are not bystanders, but calm ambassadors for peace.

# Protect Your Kid from Becoming the Bully

In the same vein of raising kids who aren't bystanders, we also don't want to raise kids to be the aggressor. When you are outlining the behaviors you want your kids to watch for and speak up about, also state explicitly that you won't condone your kid engaging in those behaviors either.

Bullying happens for complicated psychological and societal reasons. If it was simple, we would have ended it already, but clearly there have been advantages to engaging in bullying. Our kids have seen it work for high-profile people, and that can make it tempting to lean into the powerful feelings that come with being an aggressor.

Acting as a bully can make kids feel cool; there's a lot of power that comes with the ability to intimidate another person. A differentiation that may be helpful in this conversation is the idea of a bully versus the idea of a leader. A leader can also influence other people and can be very powerful and important, but does it with respect instead of fear.

Additionally, there's a real need for accountability in conversations around bullying. A kid who bullies often places blame on the victim (think: "He's so annoying, that's why I'm mean"), which is a way to distance themselves from responsibility for their actions. "I feel annoyed by that kid and decided to be mean because of it," has more space for behavior correction because there is ownership there.

If you learn your kid is acting the bully, it's uncomfortable. You've worked hard to teach them empathy, and this is what they've chosen? But it's not necessarily a reflection on you if they've slipped into that behavior. Good, smart, generally nice kids can be bullies. However, it is a reflection on you if you know it's happening and don't step in. If you learn your kid is the bully, you need to have straightforward conversations about your expectations. You might need to get some professional support. You want to actively monitor to make sure they don't have access to weapons or social media that can escalate the interactions to life-or-death outcomes. None of us truly controls the decisions our kids make, but we do owe it to ourselves and other parents to do our best to monitor and address the behavior of bullies.

# Teach Your Kids to Be Responsible About Drugs and Alcohol

Because safety. Because social media. Because severe consequences. Because hangovers.

Substance use is complicated and a constantly evolving belief system for many people. What was okay in college might not feel okay once you have a mortgage, you know? Being honest with kids about the struggle might be the best place to start. The Red Ribbon campaigns of our youth, which relied on scare tactics and worst-case scenarios, have been shown to be garbage ways of talking about substance use, so let's take a new tack and give young people real conversations about substance use and the ways we can engage responsibly.

The guidelines you want for your family around alcohol and drug use will be very personal and unique. As you're forming these guidelines, here's a few things to consider: your own relationship with substance use, the laws and consequences for substance use in your state, the risks and rewards as you see them, and general risk-reduction plans to make use as safe as possible.

One of the time-honored ways to take the fun out of substance use is to not make it excitingly forbidden. Bonnie and Faith live in Texas where it is legal for parents to let their kids drink, but be sure to check your local laws—you might be surprised! As Faith's kids got older, they were allowed a glass of wine at a family dinner or a hard cider at a family picnic. This has made alcohol something else that is out there and available and fine in moderation. Faith's son was invited to many 21-and-over events before he was 21 because people knew he wouldn't drink without permission and wouldn't overdrink because, for him, it wasn't an exotic, naughty thing. If having beer isn't something that only happens on Forbidden Planet, then the temptation to have ten beers instead of one isn't as high.

Bonnie's kid obviously isn't allowed a glass of wine at dinner yet, but is already getting lessons in moderation and responsibility by watching her parents. Faith's father is a person in long-term recovery, so while he didn't drink, he made a point of discussing why he didn't drink and encouraged his kids to have a healthy relationship with alcohol (unless they found that they couldn't). He didn't want them to fear it because he is a recovering alcoholic. So if you have an alcohol-free house, you can still have the conversations, pointing out what you notice in other homes, in restaurants, on TV, etc.

Okay, what about drug use though? Deep breaths. Obviously the answer is a hard no, and it remains a hard no until they are at least 73 years old. Except it doesn't really end up working out that way, does it? And we have to have those conversations, too.

What's out there, what's intriguing, what is dangerous, what consequences could occur, etc., etc.

You can discuss recreational drug use without lecturing, right? Even if your hard line is "just say no," you still don't want to shut your kids off or down, just as with drinking. Discuss why your answer is no, discuss ways to turn down drugs when someone offers them, always keep the door open for further conversations, *and* keep the door open in case something happens. What if they decide to use anyway, and they end up high as fuck and stranded somewhere? If you've kept an open dialogue, hopefully they call you to come get them and they stay safe.

Bonnie works with several families that have experienced that scenario; a few of them had a code word that signaled, "I need you to come get me right now and don't ask questions please." There would be time to debrief the situation later, once everyone was safe and accounted for, but those kids knew that they could contact their parents and get the help they needed without a lot of drama. This way, no one feels they have to hide those decisions; there's room for mistakes and conversation. Faith's kids grew up with the rule that telling *always* gets you in less trouble than not telling. And she would always eventually find out.

Okay, what if you use? And your kids know it? Take a deep breath and explain. Maybe you use edibles for sleep and they are legal when you do. Explain how and why you take them and that doing so is legal for you and not for them. Or if you are using something that isn't legal and they know? Then we get into the "How come you can and I can't?" Maybe it's the same edibles. Or you are microdosing to manage depression. Whatever. Explain that that's a choice you have made for your adult self with benefits that you have weighted against possible consequences.

And explain that they can make those same choices when they are also adults, but that using now may actually end up with significant legal consequences, while waiting until adulthood might mitigate those consequences (like a minor in possession charge for alcohol that could be expensive to deal with, but would be not relevant to someone old enough to legally consume alcohol).

Or, for example in San Antonio where Faith and Bonnie live, THC is illegal at the state level, but the local police chief decriminalized carrying a little for personal use without a Texas Compassionate Use Program card. This de facto "turn the other way" rule doesn't apply to kiddos. A kid holding will absolutely end up entangled in the child-serving system.

Further, those consequences could extend to the adults in their lives because the adults would be held responsible for allowing access to drugs or alcohol. You, the parent, could quite easily end up in the justice system because of their drug use, and they could end up in foster care—it sucks, but it happens. At least in Texas. And it's okay to own, "I don't have a personal problem with you using $X$, $Y$, and $Z$, but the state does, which means my obligation to you is to say no. When you're grown, you can take all of our conversations about risks and benefits and make your own decisions. Right now, I'm the decider."

How much use of alcohol and drugs is too much? That conversation is so different for every family, based on personal histories, value systems, and societal norms. Professionally, Bonnie and Faith are in the "risk reduction" camp. We try to encourage people to know their limits, stay within them, and be safe about whatever level of chemicals they want to engage with. But we work mostly with adults whose frontal lobes are mature enough to think through those complicated levels of nuance and responsibility. So how do we as parents talk with our kids about that idea?

Here are some areas to explore to help you define your own feelings around substance use and add to conversations as appropriate for your family:

- What are your own experiences with drugs or alcohol?

- What is your current relationship with those substances?

- Do your own levels of usage feel manageable and recreational, or could you be safer if you cut back a bit?

- What's your family history (if you know it) of substance use?

- Do you have your own traumas and issues around seeing loved ones struggle with substances?

- What are your fears around substance use?

- Do you even believe in recreational use as an idea?

- What are your kids asking about substance use?

- What experiences are they having or witnessing?

# Talk About School and Community Violence

Some of the neighborhoods where we raise our kids see a lot of gun violence. Even if it's rare where we live, though, the threat of school violence is everywhere in our culture. It's one of the top concerns of parents in many surveys, and our kids are being taught active shooter drills in school.

How do you talk to your kid about the threat of imminent violence? Especially if it's something that terrifies you?

Maybe it's helpful to look up the statistics on the likelihood. Maybe it's high, but maybe it's not as high as you think, or not as statistically dangerous as doing other things you take for granted every day, like driving a car. Not that statistics really help us feel better when something terrifies us.

So what are the actions you can take in this arena that are within your control and will be helpful? One approach is to teach your kid to be observant of the behaviors of others. If they see something, they need to say something to a trusted adult. According to data about school shooters published in 2024 on the Sandy Hook Promise website, 93 percent of attacks were planned prior to being carried out. Additionally, it's estimated that in four out of five acts of school shootings, at least one other person knew of the plan in advance. If our kids see something concerning, they need to pursue it. If they aren't being taken seriously, then we've got to pursue it. You've already given them the lesson of trusting their instincts when something feels icky; that applies here, too. They can trust their gut feelings that something isn't right or they're not feeling secure in a space or situation. Then they can decide if they want to try or feel capable of de-escalation. But reiterate that it's totally okay to decide to just leave the situation that feels dangerous.

Further, talking about gun violence is another area to continue the discussions you've been having about racism, oppression, and mental health/suicide. Sandy Hook Promise's data shows this as well: Black youth are four times more likely to die by gun violence than their white peers. One in five LGBTQ+ students report being threatened with a weapon on a school campus. Girls account for 90 percent of deaths in situations of dating violence.

It is indeed imperative for our kids to feel empowered to watch for the signs of impending violence, particularly in the parts of the United States where gun laws are lax and guns are stored with insufficient safety protocols. Guns are available to students who want them.

Hate crimes and senseless violence happen because people act out of hate and rage, and that's a painful discussion to have with kids. Bonnie can remember having this conversation with her own mom on the day of the Columbine shootings. She can remember the way her mom struggled to understand for herself, and then was doing her best to help Bonnie and her younger brother process what they could. She can remember the fear and vulnerability of that conversation, and even though that was a terrible day, she can remember feeling connected to and understood by her mom because she shared her own terror and sadness. Bonnie doesn't remember the specific content of the conversation, but the authenticity of the moment remains all these years later.

Other times, bad things happen because bad things happen. Because the universe is random. Because them's the breaks, kids. Bad things don't happen because people deserve bad things, or because no one is given more than they can handle. Bad things just happen, to all kinds of people, no matter their personal circumstances.

What that means for us and our kids is that we practice empathy, and we help when we can because that's all (and everything) we can do. In his book *Man's Search for Meaning*, Viktor Frankl, a noted psychologist and survivor of Nazi death camps, said it this way: "For the world is in a bad state, but everything will become still worse unless each of us does his best." If we do our best whenever we can, the bad stuff can maybe feel less bad because we are creating a community of love to catch people when they fall or struggle or grieve.

## Talk About Online Safety

Remember dial-up? Bonnie does! She can remember the first time she heard that modem sound and the little running AOL guy showed up on the screen. There is zero chance in hell that little fifth-grade Bonnie could have ever dreamed what the internet would do to our lives, or that it would ever be accessed away from those loud modems.

Kids have phones and access to the entire internet and social media. Clients of all ages bring their social media use concerns to both Faith and Bonnie. And no wonder! How we engage online is so new, and we don't yet know all the short- and long-term effects. So discussing our individual propensities, issues, and concerns is incredibly important.

U.S. Surgeon General Vivek Murthy has stated the need for more research on social media and young people. While there are benefits to being online, like connecting with friends and showcasing creativity, there's also evidence that young people aged 10–19 face more potential negative outcomes than people older than 20.

Those negative effects are related to the interplay between brain development and the reward systems of our brains as they respond to content and notifications. For young people who are already more prone to mental health issues like depression/anxiety or eating disorders, algorithm-curated content will skew in that direction, because the things we search for are then preferentially shown in our feeds.

That can create a feedback loop where young people see more and more content that makes them feel like everyone is depressed or engaging in binge/purge behaviors. The truth is that no one is totally sure about the overall impact of social media in adolescent development.

That means a lot of the responsibility will fall on parents to set limits, check in frequently, and keep open communication to support adolescents who are navigating these online spaces. You'll want to start this conversation early and have it often; this is an ongoing dialogue as the internet changes and your child changes too. The "internet safety talk" mirrors the "safe sex/ birds and bees talk": it never ends, and requires an open-door policy on your part to help keep your kid safe as they navigate new relationships.

Many kids play on tablets and phones as early as toddlerhood. Make sure you have the parental safety controls set in ways that keep your little ones safe and on apps and websites designed for kids. Stay close by, watch what they interact with, and make commentary. Even the online spaces designed to be safe for kids can have questionable content (particularly if the site is mostly user-created content, like video streaming sites).

Also, many apps for kids have in-app purchasing available, and it's really easy for your toddler to rack up a sizable bill while they play on their virtual farm. All of y'all have heard one story or another about a kid spending thousands of dollars on Candy Crush or whatever. So, when your kid is little, be nearby and nosy.

As your kids grow, continue the conversations in age- and maturity-appropriate ways. Talk about the permanence of things on the internet (even of things that seem to be gone), how people on the internet will lie to trick them, and how sending or receiving nude photos can be a legally punishable offense. Talk about the stranger-danger aspect of the internet and how they can have a healthy skepticism of who people say they are online.

Process together what it means to participate in cyber-bullying and help them look out for friends who are in danger of being on either the giving or receiving end of online meanness. Point out how provocative or mean-spirited messages can get out of hand quickly. Make them roll their eyes with irritation over how much you talk about this. That means they are alive to roll their eyes, so we still win.

Be firm but nonjudgmental in conversations about life online. You need your kid to know that you're a safe person to come to, no matter the question. Set reasonable expectations about what your kids are and are not allowed to watch online, and explain that these boundaries are to keep them safe and to make it so they don't see things they aren't ready for and cannot unsee. Talk about the pros and cons of social media and how to evaluate what they are posting. Questions like, "Would you want that post read back to you in a job interview or in front of your class full of friends?" can be helpful determinants of the appropriateness of posts. Did you know the Library of Congress, up until 2017, kept and cataloged every tweet since the inception of Twitter? Yeah, internet stuff doesn't go away.

Further, the ability to verify the people we interact with on the internet is pretty difficult. Adolescents need to learn the potential signs of being scammed or targeted for trafficking or abuse. It can take a lot of skepticism to stay safe online.

Being responsible online also means we manage our time there appropriately. Time away from their dinging notifications is important—screen time can affect sleep patterns and ability to focus. Help your kids set reasonable limits for the ways they interact electronically, and also reassess on a regular basis to make sure those limits are working as needed.

Consider your current feelings about the internet in your family:

- What time limits do you feel your kids might need to manage their online time?

- Are you okay with more time online in one area (maybe chatting with friends or playing collaborative games) versus other areas (like mindless games, social media, or streaming sites)?

- How will you enforce or encourage responsible use?
- Are you yourself engaging in responsible use?
- How do you want to talk about the benefits and dangers of being online?

## Promote Media Literacy

How many conversations have you had that started, "I saw this thing online . . ."? As in, "I saw this story online about how bats can really turn into vampires, and the lamestream media is just covering it up because they work for the vampires. Can you believe that?"

No, Cindy, we can't believe that. Because it's clearly nonsense. But with other stories and topics, it can be harder to tell what's real and what's vampires.

This is seriously getting pretty challenging. It used to be easier to tell what sites are a rando's blog versus a reliable news source. But more and more rando blogs are made to look like those legit sources, and it's easy to fall into them as fact. With the addition of incredibly powerful and adaptive AI tools, misinformation will be increasingly harder to identify. Media literacy in all areas is going to become more challenging and more important all the time. Because all media has a bias, it's useful to help your kid look at different newspapers to understand the bias in action. Political cartoons, books, TV shows—these are all places to explore and practice media literacy.

Online misinformation is incredibly powerful. It can reach large numbers of people, be passed around easily, and be made to look exactly as someone wants it to look. We've seen it come into play in elections, in stocks, and in managing a pandemic;

people will believe what they want to believe and if it looks real, it might as well be real. And as we all spend more and more of our time online, the power of this information grows because it's more likely to make its way to our ever-present screens.

Some general questions to help our kids start to navigate this might include, "Who wrote this story? Who benefits from the information in it? Can I find similar information on different sites? What does the librarian think about this website?"

Gauge your own media literacy and how you want to talk about it:

- How will you guide your kids through the process of finding real information on the internet?

- What process do you use for yourself?

- How do you stay on top of the ways that propaganda and image manipulation show up in your digital life?

- How will you manage if your kids are engaging with propaganda or misinformation?

# SEX AND CONSENT

*T*alking about sex with children-people can feel nauseating and terrifying. Bonnie used to work as a health educator on a teen pregnancy prevention project. That job involved talking with teens alllllll day about safer sex, healthy relationships, good boundaries, and birth control options. That meant demonstrations about proper condom use, and one time, Bonnie had to say the sentence, "Let's agree we aren't going to throw the condoms at each other!" Because teenagers are ridiculous sometimes, and condoms are hilarious, but also, ew. At least blow up the condom like a balloon before throwing it at your friend; don't just slime each other with pre-lubed condoms!

One thing Bonnie was surprised by when she did that work was the disconnect between the teens and the adults in their lives. When adult-only classes were provided, parents confessed that they were confused about their own bodies, had no knowledge of birth control, or needed resources for their own unhealthy relationships. Those adults and parents wanted very much to keep their kids safe in romantic/sexual relationships, but did not feel equipped to have the necessary conversations. When teens were asked about where they preferred to get information about sex and relationships, overwhelmingly they said they wanted to hear what their parents and parental figures thought about those topics.

Basically, a lot of teen pregnancy prevention work is about equipping parents and reassuring them their teens want to hear from them. So, Bonnie and Faith are here to reassure you . . . your kids want to hear from you on this topic. They want your guidance and humor and knowledge (in age-appropriate ways, obviously). They want to know they can ask you questions and not be judged. They don't care if you don't have all the answers; they want an open door and a safe space.

Faith and Bonnie both focus a lot on sex and intimacy in their practices, and we see adults struggle with these topics because of the shame they carry from the ways they learned about sex in their youth. As parents, we can help make sure our kids can have healthy, safe, and shame-free sex when they are ready for it by having regular and open conversations throughout their childhood and adolescence. Like with substance use, sexual relationships are gonna happen for most people: and in the case of your kids, probably before you, the parent, are ready. Therefore, let's do our best to help our young people have safer sexual relationships that are full of good boundaries, consent, and respect.

Here are some guidelines:

- Frame discussions in a way that doesn't make presumptions about gender or sexual orientation. Use neutral pronouns (they) and terms (partner), giving children and youth space to articulate their identities.

- Articulate an attitude that sexuality and sexual exploration (both solo and partnered) is normal and healthy, and how rules regarding sexual behavior are designed to promote safety and protect the boundaries and comfort level of others (as well as follow laws, rules, and standards of human decency).

- Have an open-door policy regarding conversations about sex. Provide a space that is shame-free and open to discussion.

- Find ways for individuals to have private time for solo exploration. Normalize this experience in conversations.

- Teach consent and boundaries and model these behaviors in all your interactions.

- If you mess up, apologize and correct. How we model taking responsibility for our actions is the best teacher for showing children and youth how to do the same when they make mistakes.

A key focus of feminism for years has been making consent mainstream. Sexual violence, coercion, pressure, and fear have dominated sexual relationships for a long time, and feminists have worked hard to shift that narrative toward safety, consent, and pleasure for all people. Even for us adults, these ideas can be challenging because we might have grown up with messaging about sex as something to fear.

We've all had to do some level of deconstructing our understanding of sex and the shame that can accompany it. Many of us are healing from sexual traumas; current 2024 estimates from anti-sexual violence organization RAINN are that every year, there are over 400,000 Americans over the age of 12 who experience rape or sexual assault. Child sexual abuse statistics are also very frightening, with thousands of children under the age of 18 experiencing abuse every year in the United States. We may be scared for ourselves and scared for our children, but we can turn that fear into action and education.

# Start Talking About Sex Early and Keep Going

Afraid your kids will have sex too soon if you talk to them about it? Take it from two sex therapists . . . the opposite will be true. For Faith's kids, sex was just another part of being human. There was nothing naughty or taboo about it, so using it as a way of rebelling didn't happen. Both of her kids expressed comfort with setting their own boundaries because they felt those boundaries were supported.

For example, Faith's son went to his first dance in sixth grade with his sweetie at the time, who was an eighth grader. She wanted to make out at the dance, and he said, "Okay, kissing. But no tongue kissing because I'm not old enough for that yet." He also made sure her best friend, who was dateless, got to hang out with them, and they pooled their money to make sure everyone got snacks at the dance. This wasn't stuff that was discussed before the dance; it was all a product of the standards set for respect and boundaries and care for others within his family. He totally got it and decided for himself no tongue kissing. And being inclusive. And cheerfully shared all the details. Things that made his momma so proud.

To help facilitate this kind of open communication, keep age-appropriate materials out and available. Rather than foist those materials upon your kids as they get older[6], just have some resources out in the main living areas.

So how and when do you actually have these conversations? There's no one-size answer to this question, so it's really about what feels authentic for you. Considering what you know about your kid and your assessment of the need for the information, what fits you? It's okay to wait until your kid starts asking questions, and it's also okay for you to kickstart the conversation. Some kids are really curious about bodies and will start thinking about all of this early, but almost every kid will start thinking about it when puberty is on the horizon. So, at a minimum, it's a good idea to begin talking about bodies, sex, and relationships sometime around puberty, because most kids have a lot of questions and they will hear a lot of misinformation at their lunch tables. The good news is, there are tons of cool and

---

6 Reading *Where Do Babies Come From?* out loud at bedtime works great with a toddler . . . reading *Not Your Mother's Meatloaf* out loud at bedtime isn't gonna work with a teen.

informative books about puberty that you can give your kid or leave lying around. (Bonnie got some books about periods at a banned-book sale, and that's what finally convinced her kid to read about puberty! No one's gonna tell that kid she can't read a book.)

There is an art to asking a teen about their dating life. Faith has found it works better in the car (teens hate parental eye contact!) and with a "So, talking to anyone new?" as an opener. Is it possible to overdo it? Sure. Respect your kids' boundaries the way you want them to respect other people's boundaries. If they say, "Dude. I got it," then totally let it go.

For smaller kids, it's both easier (no sex life yet) and harder (because you're setting the standard for the sex-life stuff coming later). When Bonnie's kid was a toddler, these conversations mostly looked like naming body parts with correct names, talking about body safety and consent, and avoiding assumptions about future romance or life paths. Bonnie's daughter knows that a vulva is called a vulva and a vagina a vagina. She knows that people like her teachers might help her keep those areas clean, but that is the extent of what should be happening there. When she asks questions about marriage or relationships, Bonnie usually says, "Someday you might meet a person you'd like to marry. That could be fun!"

As her daughter came into kindergarten and first grade, she suddenly got super interested in the idea of "boyfriends" and who is dating in her classes. Because she already had a good base understanding of consent and the different ways relationships can form and look, she's now able to have fun with these explorations instead of feeling confusion or even shame for being interested in relationships and crushes. It's important to note here that every kid will go through sexual and relational development at slightly different times, and a few will never develop sexual desires. As your kid goes through elementary school and gets into middle school, they may be ready for more explicit discussions of sex and relationships.

Ideally, your kids go to a school with a thoughtful and comprehensive sex education program that teaches them about refusal and negotiation skills and helps them identify sexual pressure. But we all know there's plenty of places where that's not the norm (ahem, TEXAS), so it's important for you as a parent to feel empowered to fill in the gaps, both factual and values-based, to help your kid navigate this sensitive time.

At every age, be open to questions and be ready to answer them. Or find someone who can. Faith always offered her kids other adults to talk to if her kids were uncomfortable with talking to her about certain topics. (Sometimes you need to check in with someone who has the same operating equipment, you know?) Our general rule is if the answer to a question includes really needful information, it's simply answered. If it is kind of a silly question, Faith goes with, "I'm happy to answer that question, but you can never unknow it." She and her son were discussing his horror at finding out what bukkake and a dirty Sanchez was. He is far more likely to say, "Nah, I'm good. Nevermind," at this point.

# Teach Healthy Boundaries Around Masturbation

As parents, we sometimes forget that our silence on a subject can appear as disapproval. And the crap we heard from our families is easily passed down to our kids if we aren't super aware of those messages.

Faith and Bonnie have both worked with so many people over the years that grew up in loving, supportive homes yet still got many negative, shaming messages about masturbation.

Masturbation is very, *very* normal, and the healthiest and safest way for all of us to explore our bodies and our sexuality. Children will start touching their genitalia as soon as they realize that it is something that exists for them to touch. We should remind them that this is something we do in private (in their bedrooms or in the bathroom), but that doing so is completely okay.

Masturbation is a good tool to manage sexual desire and navigate our own bodies. It helps us understand that desire waxes and wanes at different times. Nobody owes anyone sex— our sexual desires are our own and not the responsibility of others.

We recognize this is a complicated topic for parents to navigate. Most of us likely have a private but complex relationship with masturbation. But we encourage you as a parent to engage with this topic because, for many kids, their experiences with masturbation will be their first experiences with sex at all. And if parents tread lightly, these experiences can be shame-free and pleasurable, which sets kids up for a lifetime of shame-free pleasure.

You may want to start early with discussions about privacy. Something like, "We all do things in the privacy of our rooms or bathrooms that other people don't need to be a part of. But even private things need to be safe, okay? So if you have questions or whatever, let me know!"

As you think about how you will talk about this subject with your kids, consider the following questions:

- What are the messages you received about masturbation?
- Do you have religious or cultural beliefs related to masturbation?

- What messages are you consciously or unconsciously sending to your kids about the subject?

- What messages do you want them to get from you about masturbation?

- How can you normalize understanding desire and fantasy in ways that feel appropriate for you?

# Make Everything About Consent

If one more person tells Faith that active consent takes all the fun and mystery out of sexual relationships, she may lose her shit in a very public way: keep your eye out for news reports about some small, crazy bitch screaming from the roof of a very tall building, okay?

Active consent is sexy as hell when done right. And, shit . . . if some of the fun and mystery is taken out but that also means the rape is taken out, Faith and Bonnie are down for that exchange. Conversations about consent are a hallmark of thoughtful people; assessing comfort and interest levels are powerful skills that will be useful in many areas of life.

Conversations about consent exist in all parts of our lives, not just in the sex parts. Younger kids can learn about consent by controlling who they hug and when. Or they may learn about consent when they try to pet the cat and Whiskers scratches the hell out of them. "Kitty doesn't consent to petting right now!" was a very common phrase in Bonnie's house when her daughter was a toddler. Living things have free will; respecting consent means we give freedom to exercise that free will.

As kids grow, make it a norm to consider questions like the following: Who do you hug, and when? What level of physical touch is comfortable in a given scenario? How do you know the other person is consenting at the same level? One nice thing about coming out of the COVID-19 pandemic is how people now ask, "Are we hugging?" instead of just going in for the hug. Basically, make clear that consent is asking and respecting the answer before any move is made. When you're talking about consent, discuss how silence doesn't equal being okay. We need to ask for active assent in some way, shape, or form (whether that means nodding or a, "Fuck yes, don't stop!").

Therefore, conversations about consent need to define terms like pressure or coercion. They need to include discussions about consenting while using substances, like, what level of drunk is still okay for active consent? Also important to discuss is how people can consent at the beginning of an interaction and then change their mind at any point, and so we ask for consent frequently throughout an encounter.

One of the best ways to teach your kid about consent is to model it yourself. Consent means saying, simply, "Is this okay with you?" and checking in continuously to make sure things remain okay. With your kids you can start by saying, "Can I sit on your bed?" when you're talking to them in their room. Or saying, "You look like you had a rough day, would a hug help?" rather than just grabbing them because you see they are red-eyed and sniffily.

And also letting them know you will protect them, yourself, and those around you in more emergent situations. Meaning, even in a high-consent household, sometimes you have to make a quick decision and ask for forgiveness later. Faith's son may be a fully grown 24-year-old man, but she still put her arm out and moved him forward when he nearly walked backward into another human at the grocery store the other day. Just like she had to grab him and his trike off the road in a swoop when he decided to blast his way down the driveway at age three.

# Teach the Difference Between Flirting and Harassment

Help your kids understand that flirting requires consent. Flirting is a two-way conversation; it takes nuance and attention to detail. Harassment is overt and obnoxious. It's the difference between being tickled pleasantly with a feather and being whacked in the head with a textbook. So talk about intent versus impact, and how what seems okay for your kids might be really uncomfortable for someone else. For example: "When you snuck up on me and licked my hand, you thought it was just a funny joke. Your intent was to be funny. But it felt really yucky for me; your impact wasn't funny. Instead, it made me feel gross. Please don't do that again." Discuss how there are places where consent for flirting would be possible, like on a date but not in a workplace. Bonnie is married to a teacher, and he talks frequently about the flirting/harassment he sees in high school hallways. There's such a thin line between welcome flirting and unwelcome harassment, and part of navigating that is helping our kids recognize the need to tread lightly.

What's flirting for one person is harassment for another. What starts as flirting can morph into harassment. Our kids need help navigating this. Honestly, this conversation has to be ongoing and has a lot of room for thinking out loud and working through misunderstanding. A lot of grown-ass people have trouble with these concepts. Start by asking your kid what they see among their friends or in school hallways or what they've experienced themselves, and go from there. Go gently and with an open mind.

If your kid tells you they're being harrassed, or you think they might be, start by asking them about their lives at the moment: What is going on? Anything bugging them? Talk to them about what harassment means and what is not okay behavior from others in their lives. Then, ask if anything like that is happening. If they insist that everything is fine, leave the door open by saying, "I'm glad! If that changes, you know I got your back." If they tell you about something that needs to be addressed? Help them address it. Be their advocate. Show them how to use proper channels for resolution at their school, their scouting troop, etc. Speak clearly and factually about the incident. Be firm and calm about needing it to be resolved. Don't make personal attacks about the others involved—speak to the behavior and impact only. The U.S. government's bullying prevention website (StopBullying.gov) is as cheesy as any other government website, but has great info about legal protections that may help you advocate for your kiddo.

And if your kid is accused of harassment? Treat it just as seriously. Our sweet, precious babies who have never done anything wrong in their lives...might have done something wrong. Get their perspective on the situation. Help unpack what led to their actions (they saw it on TV and thought it was funny? Their friends convinced them? They just reallyreallyreally hate this other kid and didn't know how to handle it skillfully?) Set them up to take accountability. Whatever consequences happen at school/legally/with you at home/etc are going to help them learn a different way of interacting in the future.

One of the hardest things Faith has done as a parent is not rescuing her kids from the consequences of their behavior when it was ratchet. Instead of writing a check to make problems go away, she let her kiddos face things head on. Yes, she is being deliberately vague because she is also protective of her kids' privacy. She didn't leave them hanging in the wind, they dealt with some stuff with her by their side but without her saving them. And they learned. And they didn't repeat the behaviors.

# Make Safer Sex a Priority

Birth control is such a pain in the ass, especially if you are someone with a uterus and are sensitive to hormones. Anyone who has a generative organ and a latex sensitivity can struggle too.

Talk with your kids about options, both long- and short-term. This conversation needs to start early (probably earlier than you think it should) because you want your kid to be covered for pregnancy prevention before they start having sex. The conversation about birth control will likely coincide with the onset of puberty, although your kids don't need to be actively on a birth control option at that time. Just plant the seed that, "Oh hey, you're really growing up and pregnancy is a thing that can happen, and there are ways to prevent it! Open yourself up for the questions, help them meet with their pediatrician, and plan to give them solo time with the doc at that visit. Your doc might know, too, of some community programs or spaces where your child or teen can learn about and talk about birth control with a trained sexual health educator. There are also great websites, written for and by young people, where your kid can get medically accurate information about birth control options.

It may turn out that your kid never engages in the kind of sex where they have to worry about pregnancy prevention. But you might not know that as early as when you need to start the birth control conversations. Even if your kid does come out as lesbian or gay at an early age, conversations about birth control are still vital. Sexuality is fluid, and at thirteen, they may think they are only into dudes, but then at fifteen they meet a dreamy girl, realize they might be bi, and now birth control could become necessary—or they're still only into dudes, but the love of their life is trans. And even if they live lives where birth control is never needed, at least they have a good understanding of the options and can help friends by sharing that knowledge. There's so many reasons to talk about birth control. So go talk about birth control! But go gently and with an open mind.

Some years ago, Faith brought her older kid and bonus daughter to the gynecologist. They both were looking at birth control options, and Faith had discussions with both of them about the options and what protection each option gave (e.g., no babies, STI prevention, etc.). The gyn was so impressed she asked Faith to have the same conversation with her kids. She apparently hadn't done so and loved hearing how Faith discussed these issues. Faith was really surprised and hadn't really thought about how difficult that conversation can be for parents . . . even if you are a vagina doctor.

Cue 2017. Bonnie and Faith (along with their friend Aaron who is an MD on a college campus and therefore has lots of experience with STIs) wrote a zine about this, the *STI FAQ*. It's become a zine that parents are buying for their kids because the information in it is really pragmatic and in a manageable size. Basically, if these talks gross you out, or you don't know all the details, find a good resource. Whether it be our zine, a similar book or zine, a trusted friend or family member, or a good YouTube channel. Bring your kids to a treatment provider if you don't have the skill set to answer all their questions. Faith has done psychoeducation (therapist term for sharing useful information) with several teens and preteens in her practice at the request of their parents.

Consider: How do you plan to handle it if your kid does contract a sexually transmitted infection? What will be your process for getting them regular checkups and testing? What if they experience an unplanned pregnancy? The answers to those questions might be complicated for about a bazillion reasons.

First, depending on your state, there may be laws related to all this business. In Texas, the age of consent for sex is seventeen, but the age to consent to medical procedures is eighteen. Also in Texas are a bunch of draconian abortion laws, sex-education laws, and access to sexual–health care laws. So there is a possibility that you'll need to know what the laws are and what community organizations are available to help you navigate your local landscape. The National Network of Abortion Funds has good info about a lot of these topics.

Whatever path you'd like for your family to take through an unplanned pregnancy, you're gonna need support. Abortion, adoption, raising a baby . . . none of these are easy for young people, and each option comes with complications. What organizations are near you that could be useful? And now that you know about them, how can you support their efforts? Even if your kid never needs those services, other kids they may know are using them. In the course of their life, your kiddo will definitely hear about these needs from others, and you want them to be prepared to share accurate information.

# Teach Street Smarts

Sexual assault can happen to anyone, no matter how careful or smart they are. But you can also teach your kid street smarts that can lower the statistical likelihood that they're going to end up in a situation they can't get out of.

Teach them to trust their gut, support them in saying no and leaving situations even when it's socially awkward or someone's really trying to convince them to stay. Teach them to recognize and resist coercion; they don't owe sex to anyone just because they agreed to a date or someone got them a gift. Additionally, give them guidance that will empower them to keep an eye on their friends and stay in groups. Many parents also opt to use tracking on mobile devices, so they can check in on kids or find them quickly if needed. Because alcohol is often a factor in cases of sexual assault, it's also important that your kids understand their limits and how to keep themselves safe when it comes to alcohol.

Dr. Faith's son was probably fifteen when she and Mr. Dr. Faith took him to a local bar to hear a band they all liked. Her son ended up getting two great life lessons that night. One was about the danger of getting stupid drunk (he saw someone fall over into the street and nearly get himself hit by a car along with his friends who were trying to get him out of the street), and the other lesson was about how not to get roofied.

After they ordered their drinks (Cokes[7]), Faith showed him how to hold his glass with his hand over the top and told him that if he ever leaves it unattended, to consider it unsafe to drink and toss it. He thought it was a joke, but they discussed what roofies are, how they would impair his ability to consent to sexual activity, and that men can be victimized just as easily as women. He still holds his glass like that, though he rolls his eyes when he does so.

Generally, to avoid getting substances added to our drinks, teach your kids to keep their drink with them at all times. They'll want to cover the top of it, just like Faith's son. They should get their drink directly from a bartender or server. They can stick with friends and have a system for watching each other's drinks. There's even cups, straws, nail polish, and drink test strips that change color in the presence of a sedative. Maybe someday we won't need all this bullshit just to go and have a safe drink with

---

7 This is Texas. By Cokes we mean a carbonated beverage. Sodas, pops, etc. In Texas they are all called Cokes, doesn't have to be Coca-Cola. More apologies for our state if this makes you nuts.

friends. But for now, we can teach our kids all the possible ways they can look out for themselves and their friends.

# Encourage Them to Try Out a Sexual Partner Before Committing to Them Long-Term

Did we just say encourage your kids to have lots of sex? Not necessarily.

When people are new to sexual relationships, there is a lot to navigate. The chemical interactions in your brain when you're in a new relationship are complicated as hell. Add cultural norms, pressures, wanting the fairy-tale ending, and also mashing body parts together . . . that's actually more than a lot to navigate. Before we commit to a partner in a long-term way, we need to test their ability to communicate about topics like sex and sexuality, consent, and ground-level agreements (what we like, what we don't like, what are our relationship dealbreakers, how do we define this relationship, and so on). We can encourage our older offspring to experiment and look for compatibility with another person without some romanticized lifelong commitment.

Individuals who have strong value systems in regard to sex before marriage can still experiment within their moral boundaries to make sure that the person in question is someone who they feel that spark with, can communicate wants and desires with, and enjoy being with.

# Help Your Kid Heal from Harm

What if the unthinkable happens and your kid does have an experience of nonconsensual sex, whether it's something done to them or something they've done? This can be triggering for you, horrifying in every way, and hard to know what to do with. And can absolutely lead to longer-term trauma reactions if the healing work isn't initiated.

It's helpful to share with our kiddos that a trauma reaction is a nervous system injury . . . not a mental illness. They are reacting *very appropriately* to a horrible situation. However, once the situation is over, that reaction pattern can cause more problems than it solves. And our nervous systems don't have to be on constant alert anymore. And the trauma can happen whether we are the victim or the perpetrator; many instances of nonconsensual sex are not necessarily clear-cut. There are times when one person believes an interaction was consensual and would be totally devastated to discover they misread the situation and the cues.

Normalize the process and their experiences. Another tip: ask questions that don't start with "why." It turns out that the human brain processes "why" as a combative question that leads to defensive behaviors. Instead, try, "So what happened then?" or "Any idea where that came from?" as means of getting past the defenses to the underlying issues.

As discussed in the bullying section above, help your kid advocate for appropriate measures if they are the ones harmed. The logistics of this can be incredibly disheartening as justice can be hard to come by. If we want to take legal action, for example, it can be incredibly challenging to move through that process and not be retraumatized throughout. The inclusion of police may lead to the need for other authorities who are underfunded and difficult to work with. It takes a lot of advocacy to move through the legal side of reporting sexual violence. You'll want a trauma-informed therapist to assist with processing the experience, whether you need legal involvement or not.

If you learn that your child caused harm, you'll need to work on helping them accept accountability. That may mean they have to have difficult conversations, involve authorities, or face legal repercussions. They may feel hurt and confused if they acted in good faith and learned later that they had done something nonconsensual. Work on keeping open communication, and remind them that this can be something they did, not someone they are. Most people, especially young people, can grow and learn from their mistakes and be fantastic, loving, kind, non-harming adults if they do the heavy lifting early on. We can stand by our kids in this moment, but it's important that we don't shield them from the consequences of their actions. You may want to recruit a trauma therapist that works specifically with people who perpetrate sexual violence because those professionals have the skills to help people be accountable and work toward healing.

We want to encourage you to also get the support you need. Based on statistics of sexual assault and sexual abuse frequency, lots and lots of parents have our own traumas that we desperately wished to shield our children from experiencing. To learn that we couldn't prevent this experience could be devastating. And if we learn they have perpetrated violence on someone else, it could be even more upsetting and triggering. You deserve a space to face these feelings and get support in finding some healing.

Peter Levine and Gabor Maté have both written extensively on trauma recovery, including books directly related to raising kids in environments of constant adverse events and toxic stress. There are good tools there to help inoculate them against PTSD as much as possible, and heal from it on the occasions it happens despite all our best efforts.

# WHO WE ARE IN THE WORLD

*M*aybe it's because we live in the South and Southerners are so very inundated with moralistic messages, but Bonnie and Faith have spent a ton of time talking with our kids about differences between how we see the world and others see the world. This is a hot-button issue for both of us because we both live our values through active advocacy work. So when our kids get messages that differ from the ones we are trying to instill in them, it's easy for us to become activated.

When we do get activated, it helps to remember that kids, especially younger kids, are trying to figure out where *they* stand and are often just relaying back to us the messages they've heard out in the world. We've both found, over the years, that open conversations about a range of values (and different expressions of those values) have equipped our kids to find their own moral center rather than us being one more person trying to shove a way of living down their throat. So when your kiddo comes in and says, "Joey at school says . . ." or, "My Sunday school teacher said . . ." or, "I saw on the news . . ." how do you handle that? Here are some possible scripts to move those conversations forward:

- "That's not been my experience. What do you think? What did you hear or see about other people's experiences?"

- "This is what I believe, and this is why . . . There are lots of ways of being in the world, and even when people have different beliefs, it is coming from a place of trying to be a good person. So it's not that anyone is right or wrong; it's finding out how to be a good person in the world. What does that look like for you? For what you heard and saw?"

- "It's really frustrating to respect other people's belief systems even when they don't respect yours. Would it be helpful to have some ways to respond so you aren't getting in arguments with them or being told you are bad/wrong/going to hell? I find it's helpful to say things like, 'That sounds like something we are going to have to agree to disagree about.'"

It's really helpful to give your kids concrete examples that contradict the negative messages they are being inundated with, if you can do so without violating the privacy of people they know. Over the years, Faith has pointed out how many loved and respected people in her kids' lives were part of stigmatized communities: such as being gay, being trans, being atheist, having criminal records, or managing chronic mental illness, joblessness, or homelessness. She did this to show them that there are so many ways of being in the world that fly in the face of every stereotype they were being fed. It's useful to do this frequently because the messages our kids are getting about what is "normal" or "acceptable" are relentless.

To stand up to that deluge, we've got to be the contrarian voice, as gently and frequently as we can. Faith and Bonnie have both found it helpful to do their own homework in this regard so they could discuss issues factually with their kids. Especially as they get older, it's helpful to be able to thoughtfully discuss what the Bible really *did* say about homosexuality. Or that research shows that most people experiencing homelessness actually work full-time jobs and are not lazy.

But it's really, *really* hard to combat negative messages when they are coming from family members that you love and spend time with on the regular. Some dumbass kid on the back of the bus, or that one teacher at the school, is far easier to ignore than a grandparent, aunt, or cousin that is a lovely human being in so many ways . . . except that one belief system that regularly makes you throw up in your mouth. In moments like these, Bonnie reminds herself all the time that Bessel van der Kolk (famed trauma therapist and all-around sage person) says that well-functioning people are able to accept individual differences *and* acknowledge the humanity of others.

It's okay to say that you love someone in your family or friend circle but don't agree with them on that particular idea. It's important to honor the fact that they came to the conclusion that they did based on the messages they have received throughout their lives and their personal experiences, and that yours have been different. It's also great practice for our kids (and, ahem, ourselves) to have dialogues with individuals with whom we disagree without yelling or baiting. Even if your family member is unable to engage this way, you can continue to model this behavior on your part (back to, "That's not been my experience. Tell me about what your concerns are.").

No one is ever truly argued into a different stance. They may be argued into submission, but it will be submission with resentment. It's not that people resist change so much as they resist being changed. Research on the people who have left QAnon, for example, shows that people changed when confronting their own personal disillusionment with the movement or movement leaders. Not because someone they loved successfully argued them out of their red-pill advances. Therefore, it's important to show your kids how being a kind and loving human is what will start to shift the perspective of those around them, far more than any awkward fighting at Thanksgiving.

# Use Current Events and Pop Culture as an Opening

What are some practical ways to get talking with kids about values and their place in the world? Pop-culture touchstones are a great place to start.

Pop culture itself is typically thought of as mass media and is most frequently aimed at younger people. That alone makes it prime conversation ground because it might be stuff you don't understand or that hasn't been directly marketed to you as a parent. You can scan websites or the news to learn about the latest stuff and then sound really cool when you're like, "So I heard a story on *NPR* about TikTok and the ways it works to create community." And your kid will definitely roll their eyes at you—but it's easy to follow that up with some questions like, "What do you like on TikTok? Have you learned anything interesting there? I heard there are some therapists using the app to teach grounding techniques. That's pretty interesting!"

Movies and TV shows are also reliable moments for these types of openings. Story lines are often written to have some reflection of real life, so they can open up conversations about presence or absence of diversity, use of tropes, what happened versus what we would do in a situation, or the ways characters can be toxic, controlling, or even abusive. Try to stick with your handy-dandy open-ended questions so you avoid sounding boring or preachy:

- "What do you like about this show?"

- "What do you think about that character/storyline/scenario?"

- "Wow, that was a major cliffhanger episode! What do you think will happen next?"

- "What do you like/dislike about the relationships in this story?"

Nowadays, there are lots of shows that work hard to reflect current events. So, using pop culture in this way can give you an in to talk about things like Black Lives Matter, abortion, politics, immigration, sex and consent, mass incarceration, poverty and classism, ableism, transphobia . . . choose your topic and find a show that can open up the conversation for you. That's why representation matters; so we can all see ourselves in the stories we consume and can carry away our own interpretations of a fuller range of human experiences.

Pop culture can also be a starting place for discussing mental health issues with our kids. There are lots of positive examples of people in TV, movies, or music experiencing mental health challenges or crises and dealing with them in constructive ways. There are also lots of controversial instances of this same idea. But any of these media examples can give you an opening to discussing a sensitive subject with a simple, low-stakes conversation about something you saw on Netflix instead of overtly poking around in your kids' life. This gentle start-up approach reduces resistance to the conversation and gives space for hypotheticals, questions, concerns, and differing perspectives.

A different but equally important issue comes when these pop-culture images start affecting our kids' internal sense of worth. We are living in a very visual world. Apps and online spaces rely heavily on visual media to drive traffic through the virtual world. Those images can be heavily altered, provocative, upsetting, or unrealistic. The problem begins when our kids start to think they have to match their online idols in literal ways that start causing body dysmorphia.

As parents, we can combat this in an important way: All the body talk we do from the start is a hugely important foundation here, combined with specific discussion about the fact that our kids' favorite stars and influencers are *paid to look that way*. Their favorite pop singer is adorable, yes, because it's her job to be adorable, her income is dependent on being adorable, and it costs a freaking fortune to be adorable. Simple statements like, "Yes, she is super cute. I'm so glad my job doesn't require me to put hours of work into my appearance every day before leaving the house so I'm always camera ready! Looking that put-together all the time is a really hard job!" can really put those ideas into perspective.

The people in power see the potential of pop culture as well, for recruitment or general heart/mind influence. If you're actively using pop culture in the ways we describe here, make sure you're doing your own research about the source and teaching young people how to separate entertainment from propaganda. Critical thinking about the messages we get from pop culture is a valuable skill. And frankly, discussions where we dissect and critically review pop culture are some of Bonnie's favorite discussions. It's a fun way to frame and talk about serious things.

# Getting Involved in Politics

Coming into your own Political Views is a lifelong process and open to many layers of influence. None of us will hold the exact same views as our parents or other role models. So we can't expect our kids to have identical political views to ours. Of course, this reality can be hard to accept as parents, but it's nothing new. Talking about politics has always been a flashpoint in families; it's the reason there are so many "It's not a family party 'til someone cries" scenes in movies and TV. The majority of us can recognize real-life scenes like these from our own holiday and birthday tables.

Even in families where people largely agree, the nuance of how we feel about the two-party system, political gridlock, making laws, and the overall role and duty of government varies. With your kids, aim to have conversations that allow for passion, for debate, and for discourse, but avoid attacking or dismissing. One of the interesting things about politics in general is that it is endlessly debatable; the key is making your best effort to keep the table, holiday or otherwise, open for ideas and respectful disagreement. So long as that disagreement is not about whether or not we should treat human beings like human beings. As long as we are centering and imparting a morality that serves to care for people instead of harm them, we're creating a positive foundation for our children.

But what does this look like practically speaking? One example: fiscal responsibility and smaller federal government were the original hallmarks of conservatism, and that's not always a bad thing. Faith and Bonnie both have conservative friends that are even more horrified than Faith and Bonnie by actions happening in the name of the political party they had been aligned with (which says a lot). Pointing out to our kids that these are people we love and respect is important. We may differ on the idea of the National Endowment for the Arts, but reasonable folks can agree to less violence and more safety for our fellow humans. Because that's not a budgetary discussion but, instead, is a fundamental support of humanity.

With that in mind, it's important to remember that democracy, at its best, is a system that welcomes everyone's input and suggestions. Local politics can sometimes fit this framework better than the federal level. Bonnie grew up in a very conservative part of Texas, and when she was in fourth grade, she wrote a letter to the mayor detailing her concerns about litter throughout the city along with a few suggestions to help improve the situation. The mayor's office called, and she got to go and have a personal meeting with the mayor to talk about it; thus began her lifelong obsession with local politics.

In college, she continued that obsession by starting a petition to ask local officials to consider the implementation of a recycling program throughout the city (which was even smaller and more conservative than the place she grew up). The petition did open the door for that conversation and allowed for a pilot program of recycling drop-off stations throughout the city. Local politicians are more likely than state or national officials to still interact in these ways, and we hope they will welcome input from our kids.

Because these kinds of changes are so possible at this level, active involvement in local politics is becoming more crucial than ever. Serious decisions get made in city halls and school board meetings, and with lack of interest and involvement, those decisions tend to reflect the preferences of a vocal minority. We can really see this process happening in Texas, on school boards specifically. School boards make thousands of key decisions for your kid, from sexual health education to library books to teacher pay. Conservatives recognize the potential in those rooms and have made a concerted effort to make school boards less progressive, even if that's not the overall will of the community. If you feel like participation in national politics is a fruitless endeavor, we hear you. Your involvement in local decision making will feel much more impactful.

You can take your kids to school board meetings, or city council meetings, or debates during election season. Take them with you to cast your ballot on Election Days; in Texas they get a little "Future Voter" sticker that hopefully will hold true (both that your kid will vote and that Texas will fail in suppressing their vote). Our influence is precious and involvement in local politics is a powerful place to exercise it and introduce our kids to how they can make a difference in this way.

Depending on your state, there may be options to be involved in state-level politics as well. You can request meetings with legislators or tour the halls of the legislature. Kids can write letters, make phone calls, or attend protests for issues they feel passionately about. They can get involved with nonprofit advocacy groups to raise money or awareness of topics and issues that are decided in government. You can also help them tune in for big moments in national politics, like Supreme Court nomination hearings or impeachment trials. Government impacts their day-to-day lives in major ways, and it's important that our kids know how it works, how it malfunctions, and how they can be involved.

## Take Your Kids to the Protest

Bring your kids to marches, political events and town halls, organizing meetings, fundraisers, meetups, and other activist spaces. In doing this, we show our kids what democracy and resistance look like, and we also advocate for greater inclusion of parents and kids in social justice movements. Many social justice events are organized by young, childless people who don't always think of ways to include parents and children specifically. We as parents can work to make every space we inhabit safe enough for our kids to inhabit with us. Bonnie's daughter totally has her own pussy hat, which Bonnie carried in her coat pocket for the whole Women's March on Washington in 2017, and Faith's son has spent his entire childhood in community action work. He was the youngest person (at only a couple of weeks old) at the Million Mom March in 2000. He was pushed in a stroller and breastfed at the end.

Bonnie's daughter got to wear that pussy hat to her first march, the International Women's Day march, and she carried her own protest sign, which said, at her request, "Happy Women's Day, I love all of you!" That memory is listed among Bonnie's prouder mama moments.

You can also look for events that are designed to be family oriented, not just Angry Protest O'Clock Time. For example, Faith was on the board of the Pride Center San Antonio. We hosted several Pride family events every year and encouraged ally attendance. Kids had a great time and got to see all the different ways people can be a family. Several times, Faith's son agreed to be the Easter Bunny for the Easter Egg Hunt held every year. Everyone was surprised that he was willing to put on a smelly costume and hug a batrillion kids while getting smeared with chocolate. He shrugged and said, "This is what we do. It's important, and it's fun." Faith is deeply grateful that's his perspective.

Still, it's easy to get discouraged and overwhelmed when talking with our kids about protest work. It feels like there aren't enough of us to be in all the places we need to be to advocate for the world we want. We are online, we are in town halls, we are marching in protests, we are fundraising, and on and on and on, and still it's not enough. And as parents, we weep sometimes. And we want our children to know enough to combat injustice but not so much to overwhelm them or scare them away from seeing all that is good in the world.

How do we find our own peace with these issues and help our children find theirs? Is it a terrible thing to go out to a movie when that money could pay for someone's medication in a developing country? Be honest with your children about everyone's struggles toward finding the middle way.

Find ways to communicate that expressing love in the world means giving the world not only our work and sacrifice, but also our laughter and joy. If the only world we show our kids is one where everything is awful and there's no fun or joy, what exactly are we fighting for? A world like that doesn't feel worth the effort. But we are fighting for a world where everyone is safer, is more equal, and has more space for joy and fun, and that is definitely worth our best effort.

## Teach Your Kids About the Man

As parents, how do we discuss something like the legal system? It's flawed and imperfect, but held up as authoritative and definitive. It's based on precedent and bias. It's staffed by a lot of well-meaning people who make honest efforts at protecting people and advocating for victims. It's also full of people who love power and control. Consequences for mistakes can be larger than life because the system tends toward "tough on crime" approaches that can seriously ruin people's lives. The system ruins some people's lives more than others, not just because it's overall broken but also because it's been designed to overreact to certain types of infractions (especially those made by poor folks, people of color, or people who are substance users).

Almost everyone will visit a courthouse at some point in our lives. We might go for jury duty, or get married or divorced, or to change our name and gender markers; perhaps you have dealings with the foster care system. Maybe you have friends and family members in prison, or your kid's friends do. You may want to discuss your own experiences with courthouses and other aspects of the system with your kid so they have some idea of how those interactions look. Similarly, your kids will one day grow into adults who need to navigate various systems and paperwork. Show them what you're doing when you have to deal with banks and bureaucracies, and involve them as appropriate.

For example, police pull-overs can be really scary. Ideally, the interaction is courteous on both sides, and everyone walks away safely. Give your kids the best chance you can for that to happen by coaching them to keep their hands in plain sight, always have their license and insurance with them, explain anything they are doing and reaching for, and to respectfully interact with the authority figure who's just pulled them over. For example, Faith relayed to her kids the story of getting pulled over and telling the officer, "I need to get that out of my glove box, and I know there is an X-Acto knife from a craft project sitting on top of everything, including my insurance card . . . are you okay with me opening my glove box?"

Make sure your kids also know their rights. It's important to be careful and respectful and all that, but it's also important that they aren't experiencing civil liberty violations in the process. Teach them their legal rights (including what information they have to give and what they don't) and how to advocate for those rights if you aren't around—by using calm and polite language with a broken-record discussion technique.

Pop culture and current events can give you an opening to teaching your kid a healthy skepticism and respect for the system. Just like Faith's earlier example of her kid watching too much *Law & Order*, messages about interacting with the legal system can be insidious and pervasive. Hold these falsehoods up to the light with your kids around, saying things like, "The writers on this show really must think only Black men commit robberies. Every episode I've seen of this show uses that same lazy trope. Have you noticed anything like that?" (Maybe without the expression "lazy trope," unless your kiddo is bougie and also talks like that.)

## Teach Your Kids to Talk to Authorities

We owe our kids the truth about the importance of using a language of respect when dealing with authority figures, even when those authority figures are awful.

The reality is that there are going to be *many* people in their lives and our lives who have unequal ideas about respect. There will be people in their lives that say, "I'll respect you if you respect me," and what they really mean is, "I will respect your personhood if you respect my authority over your personhood."

And in truth, many of these people will be in positions of power over your children at various points in their lives. And we need our children to be safe in order to survive.

Of course this doesn't mean taking the abuse and bullying lying down. And honestly, protecting our children from all the insidious ways bullying can be present in their lives is a far-reaching conversation that impacts so many areas of their lives. But when it comes to dealing with authority figures specifically, there are a few general guidelines that we all need to keep in mind as parents:

- Tell them not to talk shit to police officers, school authorities, or other individuals in power. To use ma'am or sir. Or Mr./Ms./Mx./Dr./Rev./Officer/Sergeant. (Whatever the expected markers of respect are in that situation.)

- Encourage them not to enter these situations with a chip on their shoulder. While Faith and Bonnie live in Texas and are often embarrassed about the stunts their lawmakers pull, they also live in a large and generally progressive city. Faith was active in training the local police force on respecting language within the trans and gender-nonconforming community. She can attest to how hard many of these officers are really trying to get it right. And they don't have to—they are the ones with the badges and guns. So if they are trying, we can keep trying, too. We need to give each other the benefit of the doubt as much as possible, and not presume an authority figure is intending to be combative.

- In case it turns out that someone is violating their rights and their safety, teach your children the skills they need to get out of the situation with minimum impact and damage to themselves and those around them. Follow-up can always happen later.

- Remind them that you are a safe space. And teach them who else around them is a safe space. Remind them repeatedly that you will have their back and do everything in your power to protect them. Reiterate that you are not perfect. That you may be distracted and overwhelmed by your own life, so you may not read their nonverbal cues that something is wrong. But you will immediately stop and pay attention if they say, "Something is wrong, and I need your help." Remind them that there are other people in their lives who will do the same. Ideally, you will have a point person for your kid in all of their life domains. Their school ally, home ally, neighborhood ally, sports team ally, church ally, etc., etc.

- Teach pragmatic strategies for self-protection. Get your kids enrolled in self-defense courses. Teach them basic activist first aid. Talk to them about filming interactions and show them how to download and use the ACLU app on their phone.

# Money, Money, Money

Money. We like it. We keep it in a jar on top of the fridge. We'd like to put more money in that jar.

But more importantly, money can be conceptualized as *energy*. Energy allows us to do other things we want to do. Energy is something we can share with other people. Money isn't a means in and of itself. Teaching our kids about money is teaching them how to use their energy in the world.

Start talking with them about how our society operates. You know, capitalism. And how the way it works in this country (along with other systemic social structures) has contributed to inequality. Help them learn responsible buying practices and teach them to do what good they can within the framework of capitalism. Take them to local farmer's and artist's markets. Shop local and small when you can, and show them how to barter and share. Model ways we can all use our creativity to make, DIY, upcycle, and program the things we need.

Growing up, Bonnie's dad *always* used to harp on the idea that "money doesn't grow on trees." (He had a few sayings like that, but that one was really in frequent rotation.) Little kids flat-out do not understand money. And it's hard to talk to them about it because they don't understand language like "payroll," or "budget," or "saving for a rainy day." Their frontal lobes don't understand planning ahead, and they like instant gratification. Hence the parent-tested favorite line about money trees. You, the grown-up with a budget, need concrete ways to talk to kids about this.

For example, Bonnie gives her daughter specific days when she can get something new. So if they need to run into the drugstore for a couple of things, Bonnie can say, "We are running in here for toothpaste and cat litter. There will be toys here, but today is not a buying day for toys. The next day I would consider shopping for toys is Saturday, which is three days from today." That really helps cut down the, "But I really need this random princess car that lights up!" tantrums, saves money, and keeps that stupid random princess car out of Bonnie's living room floor, only to be stepped on later. As her daughter got older, the family implemented a system of doing a few things around the house in exchange for an allowance. Now when her daughter wants something at the drugstore, Bonnie can ask her, "Do you have your money with you?" and her daughter can make the decision for herself if it's a day for buying light-up princess cars.

Studies show that kids pick up a lot of subconscious ideas about money, what it means, and what its importance is in our lives. They internalize the anger and shame that often accompany money management, and parents don't even realize those are the vibes they are passing around. So a proactive discussion about money and money management can head off those shame feels and increase your kid's overall earning/sharing/investing potential later.

Talking about money may lead to talking about career and life plans. What's your kid interested in doing? Will they need a degree or certification? How will the cost of that factor into their overall earning plans? Are they interested in something they can jump right into or maybe getting an apprenticeship and then getting going? Not all of our kids will go to college, and there are tons of cool jobs that don't require it, so why take on the cost of a degree they won't use? If money is energy, talk about ways we can invest that energy in ourselves to make the life we want, college track or not.

## Teach Your Kids About Wealth Inequality

Kids become aware, pretty quickly, about wealth inequality in the United States. Particularly when they live in a family that doesn't have a lot of wealth. And when the kids around them (in their school, neighborhood, church, etc.) appear to have wealth, your kids may have a lot of questions.

Faith remembers her kids asking if they were rich. While they lived in the same neighborhood as their friends and went to the same school, they had books to read and new bikes when they outgrew their old ones, and they had peers that were jealous and snarky about it. This led to a conversation about how families make choices about spending money. We didn't spend money on cable TV and didn't take expensive trips because we wanted to make sure our kids could play sports, ride bikes, and have good books to read. It didn't mean that cable and trips were a bad choice, just a different one.

It also led to discussions about how families can have the same levels of income but have different expenses that we may not see. Someone may have a lot of medical issues that are very expensive or a family member who is paying off student loans (Faith and Bonnie right here). Maybe their friends are able to stay with their grandma after school until their parents get home, while your kids are in an afterschool program you have to budget for.

This is where Faith was able to remind her kids that when she was in school and working part time, they got their books from the library instead of the bookstore, as well as ate meals at home far more than kids-who-want-to-go-out-for-burgers would like. Faith found that as her kids got older, these early lessons helped them see the struggles of their friends in a different light, which gave them empathy and propelled them to be helpful when they could (bringing extra food at lunch to share, letting Faith know that a friend's dad is out of work and can't afford the gym uniform and "we can help right mom?")

As our kids get older, we can have discussions about privilege and poverty and wealth disparity. We don't have to be Team Anarchy to start discussing how difficult it is for some people to rise out of poverty, and that it is not a sign of weakness or laziness to continuously struggle. And this can lead to discussions about money-as-energy instead of money as an end itself. In a world that prioritizes and uplifts wealth as an ultimate goal, here is your chance to discuss money as one of many resources in your kids' lives and to discuss balancing that resource with other resources like time, rest, connection, and relationships.

On a larger scale, discussions about wealth distribution, earning potential, and class are typically oversimplified. The language employed can be used to manipulate people into voting against their own interests when class is used as a tool of separation and competition. Because Bonnie has a lifelong love of politics, she often watched presidential debates as a kid. She can remember lots of references to "strong middle class" and the dreaded "Wall Street versus Main street" phrase that old-dude politicians love to employ during debates and speeches. Those phrases continue to exist in our language because class in America is a key part of life. The American dream is predicated on the idea that anyone can succeed; pull up on those bootstraps and make your millions!

The mythology of the American Dream exists in tandem with the fact that, for generations, policy decisions have been made with the purpose of steeping particular communities in poverty and violence. For generations, the legacy of white supremacy and classism have been key factors in policy and government decisions that have material effects on people's lives. The zip code a person is born into is a huge determinant of their access to quality health care, education, transportation, and jobs. Success in the United States is not just a matter of how hard a person works; it's a summation of generations of decisions that have brought us to this economic structure.

To begin this conversation as a parent, consider: What has class meant in your own life? Bonnie grew up with parents who worked hard, and she had the ability to do most things she wanted, but her family didn't really take vacations or drive new cars. She had friends who did those things and more, and friends who did way less, and she can remember noticing the difference in experiences around her but not really understanding what it meant. Ideas about wealth inequality and the 99 percent didn't factor into her consciousness until much later in life, but those experiences were real even without the vocabulary to discuss it.

Your kids will also notice those different experiences. It's important to be honest with kids that this is a real and emotional experience for their friends. They may have a friend group of people with mixed realities. Maybe your kid is the one who can afford the nicest prom dress; how will you teach them to be thoughtful about that privilege? Or how about if your kid is the one working to help support the family? How can they share that with pride while being honest about the stress that can accompany a tight budget?

Make sure your kid has a wide range of ideas about how to spend time that include low-cost or free activities that everyone can attend and enjoy. Teach them to be inclusive and thoughtful about access to spending money and to do so in a welcoming way, like, "Hey, my mom always buys lots of extra snacks in the summer. Want to come chill at my place and then we can head to the skate park?"

The reality of the U.S. economic system is that the majority of us are much closer to being homeless than to becoming millionaires. The system is designed to thrive when lots of people are just barely getting by. The COVID-19 pandemic exposed this reality in very clear ways, and has also shown how politicians think about support programs. In Texas, accessing support like unemployment benefits, food stamps, childcare assistance, or rental relief is complicated as fuck. During the pandemic, some of those barriers came down, but the state was waiting with bated breath to be able to make it difficult again. Do you know how to access such programs where you live? Do you think it's important for your kids to know how to access those programs?

Bonnie has been involved for many years with a nonprofit that serves as a shelter and rapid housing program for LGBTQ+ youth, so conversations about economics and homelessness have been ongoing in her home. If the family has extra cash, it goes to that organization. If they have a chance to attend events or volunteer, they do. Because of this, her daughter has had lots of conversations about the lives of people who are experiencing homelessness; she has some idea of how easy it can be to get to that place and conversely, how difficult it can be to get started from that place. She knows her family isn't a savior to the youth or the organization because there's a community of love and support around the organization. It's a group effort she's proud to be a part of.

# Climate Activism

Climate change and catastrophic weather are quickly becoming a pressing issue for every family, whether that means staying safe in extreme weather and storms, budgeting for the added costs of heating and cooling, or managing the loss from floods or fires. The climate crisis is driving a lot of the inequality we talked about earlier.

Many young people are incredibly passionate about climate activism. They see the earth changing in ways that will not benefit them, and they are scared and feel grief and anger about this truth.

But being environmentally conscious doesn't mean you have to be extreme. You're not a hypocrite if you do what you can but not everything that it's ever possible to do, and you can teach your kids it's okay to do your best and be part of the effort. But doing nothing is not an option: so what does it look like for your family to participate in climate action?

It's important to choose strategies that actually work for you and your family. Like with everything else, combine your sustainability actions by talking about why you're doing them:

- Look at the available resources in your community. Do you have access to good public transportation? Is it feasible to walk or bike your kids to school instead of driving? Does your city help you recycle, compost, or otherwise manage household waste in sustainable ways? Are there good thrift stores or buy-nothing groups in your area so you can lower your family's purchasing of new clothes or other items? How about local organizations that can use your kids' clothes and shoes, leftover art supplies, or books as your family outgrows them? Capitalism thrives on consumerism; to create a sustainably focused family is to lower your role in capitalism overall and to have less of a detrimental impact on the health of the planet.

- Teach your kids to observe the world around them. They can get a lot of information from their four senses, like about the smell of the air, the taste of water, the colors and sounds of plants. Do they make sounds? Less listen closely and quietly and see what we notice. Help them be comfortable in and appreciate nature.

- Talk about climate can be part of talking about other rules, like how we are all supposed to clean up our messes, share, etc. Lots of parents tell their kids not to waste food, water, energy, or hold the fridge door open forever. Being able to explain why, from not just a money perspective, but an environmental one, can help bring that reality home.

- Involve your kids in choosing and doing family projects or challenges. For instance, see if you can spend a month eating local produce with every meal, adjusting the thermostat by a few degrees, or not buying new things made of plastic. Younger kids can get really into this stuff, and some of the changes might become permanent habits.

- Encourage and support your kids' ideas around sustainability. They have good ones.

- For many families, food choices are one of the most accessible ways to take concrete action. Talk with your kids about why you eat the way you do. Maybe you're vegan or vegetarian, maybe you try to buy locally grown produce when it's in season, or maybe some foods and products are off the table because of ethical considerations around farmworker treatment or agriculture practices, or you just don't want junk food in your home. Your kids may not follow this value system when they are outside of the home. And that's okay. If anything, it will reinforce the standard you are setting. Faith doesn't keep junk in the home. Both her kids learned early on that when they ate junk elsewhere, they felt pretty crappy after.

- Look for opportunities for your family to take bigger actions. Boycotts, purposeful purchasing, phone banking or letter writing, supporting specific legislation efforts, etc.

- If climate and environmental issues are important to your kid, there are many powerful youth-led movements for them to tap into as they get older.

- Talk to your kids about climate anxiety and grief; give them tools to cope as well as taking action. As with many other aspects of activism, it can feel daunting to pause and see how much work we need to do. But it's helpful to also see all the work we have done and the creative ways people are addressing problems. When people feel climate anxiety, it can be soothing to read about ocean cleanup efforts, or learn about the people who advocate for denim recycling, or watch a video about the science of using cow poop to make fuel. Even though things are hard, there are people all over the world taking meaningful action, and we all need that reminder. Our time spent in climate activism can sometimes feel futile because the work is so big, but our efforts exist in tandem with millions of others, and that is empowering.

# DEVELOPING SKILLS FOR GROWN-PERSON HUMANING (YOU KNOW, ADULTING)

*T*he word "adulting" has become overused to the point of irritation. And yet, the struggle to do these important grown-up-in-modern-society things continues to be, well, a struggle for most people. Like, "How do I put air in my tires?" or "How do I make a doctor's appointment to talk about antidepressants when I don't know how to make a doctor's appointment even when I'm not depressed as fuck?" And on the macro level, how do we make the world safer, better, and kinder when we still can't figure out the public transportation app? When we as parents teach tasks like this to young people, it means they can have more energy and brain power to devote to the bigger issues of the world.

This chapter is far from a comprehensive list of everything a human needs to know, but the good news is that you don't have to teach your kids every single thing they'll ever need to know— you just need to teach them to be responsible, and how to learn stuff they don't know. I mean, Faith just figured out how to fix her fancy-ass automated cat box using YouTube videos the other day, her PhD didn't cover the topic, and that's okay. (An added bonus? If your kids learn any of the stuff in the pages to come, they will be able to lighten your own household burdens.)

So, what can we as parents do to lay the foundation for the work of day-to-day life—in a way that's more equitable than what we may have experienced growing up? We think a simple place to start is to empower your kids to be able to manage their own day-to-day tasks. Even though this may seem pretty basic, it's powerful to teach self-reliance and efficacy. Managing your own laundry or understanding public transportation helps equalize; there's less of a privilege gap in knowledge of basic tasks, which in turn helps our kids avoid shame or embarrassment of not knowing the basics. Over time, these basics become routine, and there's peace in routine, but there's also space in routine. Once we have a solid routine, we have more headspace for the bigger issues and ideas rolling around in our heads and in society. Then, as our kids take this equity into their own relationships, they are more likely to have a healthy and functional division of household, emotional, and relational labor in the future.

# Write Thank-You Cards

A thank-you note feels so rare, almost old-fashioned, which is what makes it so lovely and unexpected. It could be a note sent after a job interview (Faith once got a job she was wildly unqualified for because she wrote one), mailed in response to a kind gesture, or even just written in simple appreciation for another human. Bottom line, the world needs more kindness and gratitude, and a thank-you note is a quick and easy way to communicate those things to others. A client told Faith once, "I don't do X, Y, and Z in expectation of slavish gratitude. But when I get a recognition and a thank-you, it makes all the difference in the world to me. I feel valued and appreciated."

A thank-you note can be for anything. One year during the winter holidays, Bonnie asked her then-toddler what she would like to say to her teacher on the holiday card. She had a very lengthy treatise that boiled down to, "Thank you for taking care of me and teaching me stuff and letting me bring Tigey to school with me," and it was quite adorable. Bonnie let her write the note in the card for herself, and then Bonnie translated it for her. Her teacher cried when she read it. We don't have to teach our kids to be genuine in their thankfulness; we only need to give them opportunities to share that gratitude with others.

Thank-you emails, phone calls, or text messages are all obviously appreciated as well. Maybe this feels so important to Faith and Bonnie because they live in the South and their grannies were serious about all things thank-you. But it's an art to be able to show real appreciation to others in the world, and it can serve our kids in the long run, too. It's simple and a win-win.

# How to Use Public Transportation

Public transportation gives people the freedom to pursue a social life, the ability to work, and the opportunity to learn how to manage another societal system, which in turn helps increase their competence in general.

The ability to use public transportation is another art and an incredibly important life skill for kids of all ages. Unless you are lucky enough to live in a walkable or bikeable community, learning public transit will allow kids the freedom to get around independently even if they don't have a car or can't drive (and it's a lot safer than driving).

We are lucky in San Antonio to have a pretty decent public transit system. Looking up the routes and planning your trip are both pretty easy. So Faith taught her kids the ins and outs of this process—showing them how to navigate the bus website, pointing out the smaller details like the digit sequences specific to each bus stop (so they could make sure they were on the right side of the road), etc. She would also drive the route with them so they could see where they would get on, transfer, and get off. Even better if you can ride transit with them regularly so they can see how you handle yourself.

Bonnie did not grow up in a city with public transit and has not often needed it as an adult. As a result, she routinely feels unsure of herself when she does need to use it. A few years ago, she traveled to a protest with a friend who was really good at navigating the public transport of the city they were in. (Thank goddess for that friend, for real.) Without that friend, Bonnie would have had to just ask strangers or make a guess about which train to take, which direction to go, and what time to get on.

All kiddos are different, but Faith's kiddos were bus-trained by early adolescence. If you have a responsible older kid who will be in charge of public transport while bringing the younger kid, it's still a great idea that the younger kid has the same basic skill set so both kids feel more secure about the process.

# How to Do Basic Maintenance

Teaching your kids basic troubleshooting and repair on stuff around the house is a gift they'll use their whole lives. If you don't know how to do this stuff, you can learn alongside them. If they know what to do when the toilet doesn't flush, or their computer doesn't turn on, and when to try to fix something themself vs. when to call (and pay for) an expert, this is good.

Teens who drive should also know how to do basic car maintenance. Even if they have roadside assistance, there are basic car maintenance skills that we should all know. Adding oil. Inflating the tires. Changing a flat tire. Things that aren't difficult to do, but save tons of money (and valuable time in important situations).

The process of changing a tire is easy, but the tools can seem daunting if you're a first-timer. Show your kid how their vehicle owner's manual (or equivalent online video) has instructions for using the jack and loosening the lug nuts. Show them where the spare tire is located in the vehicle and how to release it from its holder. Have any kits or gear that would help with the process. (Faith bought flat-tire kits for everyone's cars.[8]) Let them practice in a safe and dry place so they get the process down when they aren't under the stress of being stranded on the side of the highway with a blowout.

And even if we don't ever need these skills to change our own tires, we can help our fellow citizens when they need it. Bonnie does know how to change a tire because her dad made her practice changing the tires on her 1967 VW Beetle before she could drive it anywhere. But one time, she was pregnant and got a flat tire and was going to change it herself, when a guy on a bike stopped to help. When she thanked him, he said, "Hey, sometimes you gotta do some shit from the heart." See, learning how to change a flat tire can actually make your kid a better community member!

# How to Pack for a Trip

We all have stuff. And we like to take that stuff with us when we go places. We might need it! And we don't want to buy a new one out on the road! (Yes, we know it's unlikely anyone will need our charger for an iPhone 5. But *what if?* Huh??)

Whether our kids are heading for a weekend with their grandparents or off on their first college tour, they're gonna need luggage. And not just a suitcase full of gummy bears (though on second thought, that does not sound like a bad idea at all). Our kids need to know how to think about their trip and what they will need to navigate it successfully. How to think about layering, how to plan outfits around only one or two pairs of shoes (so you aren't going all Carrie Bradshaw). How to pack extra shirts because Thou Shalt Spill. What to sleep in when not at home (hint: not raggedy shit, because what if

---

8 As well as things to help them break out the window of the car if they are stuck in a bad accident. (Faith likes pragmatic gifts.)

the fire alarm goes off in your hotel, and now you're outside a downtown Fort Worth Holiday Inn Express in some very unfortunate old boxers). How to pack mini sizes of your go-to toiletries. Knowing details like these will empower your kids to travel competently as they navigate the world.

This also applies to everyday packing. Bonnie's daughter carries a gigantic backpack to school every day, and even though Bonnie encourages her to clean it out regularly, she doesn't, and that backpack is heavy as shit. There's some evidence that this kind of inability to organize and condense for packing might be related to neurodivergence. And a neurospicy kiddo can be brilliant in many ways, but developmentally about three years behind in others. This all catches up in adulthood, but it's common to see a 15-year-old with ADHD seem more like a 12-year-old in some aspects of their lives at that point. Which is to say, consider your kid's abilities when you are trying to get them to think about packing.

Take some time to help your kids figure out what they need to carry with them. What's useful and necessary? Are they carrying those things safely and efficiently? Where are they going, and what will they actually need to get there? How do you decide what to carry around every day, and how do you modify that based on where you're going?

# How to Clean a Dwelling

The places we live get dirty because we live there. Therefore, we as humans have to learn the right ways to clean stuff so shit actually gets cleaned. (Not just dirty shit swished or moved around, or hidden for mom to find later when it's *gross as fuck*. Ahem. Not that that's happened.)

When it comes to teaching our kids about cleaning our home, it's important to remember that because everyone lives there and is making messes, everyone needs to clean. It's a way we show respect for each other and our shared spaces, but it's also important that relational labor like this is spread evenly. It can't be on one person in a home to keep everything nice for everyone else.

It can be tough to get kids to chip in on housework for many reasons. One reason is that some kids are stubborn and don't want to help. Or they're getting mixed messages within or outside the home about who should be doing what sort of work. Another issue could be your own issues about letting people help you; Bonnie is a bit of a control freak who likes things a certain way . . . so letting her kid help clean up is a practice in letting go of some expectations. If this process of letting go also sounds daunting to you, start small.

For example, little kids can help with chores, like picking up any toys they got out to play with, putting away their clean laundry, feeding pets, and setting the table. Letting them do these things helps them build confidence and pride. As they grow, give them more responsibilities around the house, like doing yard work, cleaning bathrooms, cooking (and the accompanying cleanup), and doing their own laundry. This comes with a conversation about how everyone in the home lives there and contributes in ways that serve the family unit, and we respect the time and effort of the others who live in our home with us.

Rewarding housework with things like allowances or treats are personal decisions to make within your family, but lay it out clearly for your kid so they understand the system. Most data suggest that people like to feel helpful, and for some kids, that's motivation enough, but for many others, a positive reward will add to those happy helpful feelings and get kids more motivated to help out. This is not about bribery; it's about choosing an appropriate reward for a job well done.

Teach your kids the specific processes you use in your home to clean things. Do you have a tried-and-true process for managing laundry in your home or cleaning bathtubs? If so, take your kids through the process of how you like things to be done or how you have determined works best for your home and life, and increase their chances of meeting your expectations. And . . . if they have suggestions for improvements or changes, entertain them, because maybe you don't know everything, you smug adult.

# How to Cook Five Different, Inexpensive Meals from Scratch

Feeding ourselves is a pretty basic human need. Feeding ourselves on a budget, without fast food, is a real skill. It is also a great "win friends and influence people" skill. (Almost as good as being able to tie a cherry stem in a knot with your tongue.)

Honestly, a lot of cooking skills are about preparing for young adulthood poverty. Any of us who have lived on the two-for-a-dollar tacos at Jack in the Box and *ahem* borrowed a roll of toilet paper from work, remembers what it felt like to weep with joy over a real, hot meal. Pizza isn't cute day in and day out.

Faith's older kid was pretty determined to never learn to cook. Until they got tired of eating Subway (they worked there, so it was free) and called, begging for details on putting together a pot of spaghetti.

A huge part of feeling confident in the kitchen is knowing kitchen safety. So if we're gonna let our kids hang out with us in the kitchen, they need lessons in food safety, knife handling safety, avoiding hot oil splatters, staying safe around the oven, putting out kitchen fires . . . you know, all that deadly shit that can happen in the kitchen.

We aren't ending this section with the five recipes everyone should know, because those five recipes may vary greatly from family to family. We do suggest thinking about your go-to healthy and comfortable meals. And basic cooking skills that make creating endless meals possible: like cooking grains and legumes, making veggies taste amazing, working safely with meat and eggs if those are in your diet, etc. (Once Faith's older kid realized how easy it was to hard-boil eggs, it was like the clouds had parted and the angels were singing. And for the record? Faith likes to mash her hard-boiled eggs with avocado instead of mayo. That's an official recipe right there.)

# How to Stock a Pantry with Staples and Grocery Shop like a Pro

Once a week, Bonnie's family sits down and plans the meals for the next seven days. This way, the kid gets input on what she wants to eat and she can even check the fridge to see if she needs more yogurt. They talk as a group about how the meals go together and ways they can reuse ingredients to maximize the budget and the efficiency. The kid loves to go to the grocery store because they have carts that look like race cars, and she gets to hold all the coupons. When they get home from the store, she helps put the groceries away and usually only drops a couple of things.

Bonnie includes her kid in this process for many reasons. First, she wants her to be interested in food and cooking. Second, it's important that her kiddo knows that everyone chips in on planning, purchasing, and preparing meals. Third, she looks really cute driving her race car cart and waving coupons at people.

Beyond meal planning, teach your kid to stock the pantry, so you always have a supply of pasta, rice, sauces, and canned beans and whatever shit you need for those five basic meals in the last section. Or even foods for those days where you're feeling more, "Fuck this shit, I ain't cooking, no matter how much you think it's a good idea." Keeping peanut butter and granola bars and crackers around can be a goddess-send on those days. Because sometimes you are eight cents short for the two-for-a-dollar tacos and that ain't no joke. And, let's be real, an apple and peanut butter is hella better for you than some tacos that haven't seen a price increase in over a decade and just *can't* be made with real meat.

One area of the grocery store where young people need a lot of coaching is the produce section. The joy of biting into a juicy, ripe, summer-fattened peach is a beautiful thing to share with our children. Help them experience it every summer by teaching them how to pick ripe, organic produce, and stay away from hard-as-rocks-sad-bad peaches.

It helps to have a handy list of the in-season fruit and veg for your region because they will taste better and be better in quality. There's also the "Dirty Dozen" list of the produce that requires the most pesticides to grow. And then you need all the tips and tricks for picking the best produce; for example, are you a watermelon tapper or shaker? Whatever your methods, kids love to learn that stuff because it's sort of funny to lovingly caress the avocados to find the best ones.

# How to Use a Library

Free books! Smart, revolutionary librarians! Buildings of civility and democracy! Free access to information!

During the pandemic, libraries were closed to the public, and suddenly the community could really understand all the ways libraries were helping people. Libraries offer free internet and wifi, computers, and printers, as well as fun programming for people of all ages. They are a place to cool down or warm up when the weather is extreme. A polling place for voting day. A meeting space for community discussion or crochet classes. A safe place for people to spend time after school. A quiet place to think or read or listen to new music. Clean restrooms. Summer reading programs. Free art supplies. Toddler story time. There seems to be almost no limit to what libraries offer, and no one will ask you for a dime while you're there (unless you've got late fees to pay).

We hope you take every chance you get to reconnect to your local library. Look online to see what the safety guidelines are and what programming might be happening. Take your kids of all ages and introduce them to the librarians so they know what librarians can offer, like reading suggestions or how to use the library search function. Maybe your kid can even get their own library card!

Bonnie's kid got her own library card when she was a toddler, which was a proud day but also sort of bullshit because Bonnie specifically remembers having to wait until she turned eleven to get a library card. Bonnie grew up in libraries, both public and school, and still hangs out in them whenever she can.

Libraries are wonderful community-focused spaces, welcoming and safe. And libraries have options now that didn't exist when we were kids. The one by Faith's house has movie nights and game nights. Besides the in-house story time, our local system also lets you call in to hear stories and for homework help. They have a digital lending library and a music download subscription that allows you three songs a week to download.

Because libraries are places that are maybe a little more low-key on the adult oversight/intervention, it's also a great place to let your kids wander the stacks and see what they might want to learn about on their own. Bonnie remembers being allowed to do just that as an adolescent, and it was a chance for her to find information on topics she wanted to know about but didn't feel she could talk about with adults in her life.

That also means your kid could be wandering the stacks and find some stuff that's not age-appropriate (for example, that summer Bonnie was twelve and read all of Stephen King's *It* in a cozy armchair by the window) or maybe things you really don't like or want them to read (hateful rhetoric or scary topics, maybe). That is definitely a risk, but the freedom to explore the library mostly outweighs that risk. Do your best to have a general idea of what your kids are looking for in the library, ask them questions about the books they choose or topics they research, and keep your communication open.

Because libraries are free and house a lot of valuable information, they are frequently the targets of people who believe in censorship. School districts and local libraries all over the country have been facing significant pressure to limit options in libraries, with many conservative activists calling for complete bans of certain kinds of books. NEISD (North East Independent School District) in San Antonio has been making news for just such efforts being led by a few people. (Guess which school district our kiddos were—and in Bonnie's case still are—in?) We support people's right to decide which books are okay for their own families; we don't support them making that decision for the whole community. Stay active with your local libraries so that the only voices aren't the ones who are calling for book burning, à la *Footloose*.

Also, let's talk about libraries other than the municipal ones we all think of. Show your kids other library options. Like the little free libraries popping up in neighborhoods. Or the ones created by local organizations. One of the ones that Faith really loves in her area is the one run by the local workers union (she donates her zines to them!). A lot of cool shit like this falls under the radar, so some web searches and asking other people in your area about what's available is a good start.

# How to Write a Resume/Do a Job Interview

This is seriously an art. We can all make a basic resume by downloading templates from the internet; that's how Bonnie made her first resume (thanks Google, for knowing what neither peers nor parents did in that situation). However, there are likely some people in your social circle who will help you make a good-looking resume that will stand out from the rest. Take time to find that person who's good at that design stuff, because a stand-apart resume can help your kid get a *better* first job, which means higher lifetime earning potential forever. And now that freakin' *every* job has an online application process, it matters even more. You can't just walk into a grocery store dressed neatly, with good eye contact and a handshake, and walk out with a job. We have to represent on paper to even get a shot at representing in person. And that process is becoming more difficult all the time as more major companies utilize AI screening technology to choose who to interview. If your kid is applying for jobs and not making it past the screener, encourage them to keep trying until they can find the right key to the algorithm.

Many kids will start to look for jobs around age 15. To help your kid prep for a job interview, start by helping them pick the right clothes for the interview. Then brainstorm some questions they may be asked. Toss those out to your kid, and let them fumble around with the answers until they settle on something that sounds okay for them. A few ideas to get you started:

- How did you hear about this job and what made you interested in it?

- What are your strongest qualities related to this job?

- Walk me through the steps of helping a customer at this job.

- If you could be an animal, what animal would you choose and why?

- You learn that a coworker is doing something that's against policy. What do you do?

You can start this practice much earlier than the teen years though. Even little kids love talking about jobs and work. Bonnie's daughter used to enjoy pretending with her play kitchen and cash register that she was running a grocery store/bakery hybrid. (Incidentally, the prices at her store seemed very steep; $950 for a muffin and some laundry detergent?! But you know, inflation is a bitch.) While she played, Bonnie asked her some questions like, "What's your favorite part of working at a grocery store? How did you make this delicious coffee? What makes you good at this job?" This sort of play builds kids' confidence to focus on their creativity and strengths, and that's what they'll need in a job interview down the line.

# Proper Handshake and Eye-Contact Guidelines

A good handshake is important everywhere, job interview or not, and is basically firm and not awkward. It's not a "how strong is your grip" competition nor a chance to do your best hand-puppet impersonation of a dead fish (which is the grossest thing ever, y'all). It's not a time to do a Will Smith/Fresh Prince impersonation either. Hand out, smile, direct eye contact, firm shake, let go. Also, a good handshake can help, in theory, to avoid the clumsy, "Is this gonna be a handshake or a hug?" thing because you're coming in strong with a solid handshake. (We aren't promising that the hug thing won't happen. People are cringey sometimes.)

With your kid, take time to practice business/first impression handshakes by doing the extremes (hand crush vs. dead fish), and then finding something in the middle. Eye contact should be brief but not shifty; aim for maybe five to ten seconds of eye contact and then glance around. We want our kids to find that space between *who, me?* and *trying to stare into the other person's soul.* Add appropriate head nodding so you don't look like C-3PO, and you're golden. To demonstrate this practically, stare at your kid until it feels too weird for them. Then they know where C-3PO territory begins and ends!

Cultural practices around things like handshakes are shifting and can look really different year over year. In addition to practicing things like handshakes, we can add some practice time with our kids around phone or online interview skills. It's a lot to juggle and may be more challenging for people in your family if you've got neurodivergent folks. But these skills are teachable and practicable for people all along the neurodiversity spectrum. If your kid is neurodivergent, offer them the coaching you've used to help them navigate other social scenes; you know what works for your kiddo. And if you are a neurodivergent parent, you may decide you want some backup in this discussion. It's nice to have a range of experiences when teaching something like this that can seem overly simple, but in practice, has many variables and nuances.

If you don't live with neurodiversity in your home, it's still worth a discussion about how other people may be unsure of a social interaction like this and to help kids brainstorm some ways to make this feel more natural for everyone. Bonnie reminds her daughter really often that people don't all process the same. And that sometimes facial expressions or other nonverbal cues land differently for other people, so it's nice, particularly when meeting someone new, to verbalize what she's thinking and ask for consent with interactions. Something like, "Wow, it's great to meet you! Would you like to shake hands?" is super simple and helpful. Bonnie has seen her daughter use this type of interaction at places like playgrounds and museums; "Hi! I think it looks fun to climb up to the top of this, but we need to take our shoes off. Are you okay with doing that right now?" Which tracks, because most elementary school kids aren't necessarily shaking hands. But her daughter can take that style of comfy and inclusive intro into many experiences in her life.

Once our kids have managed to practice all this, we need to talk more generally with them about how handshake and eye contact norms vary vastly across cultures, communities, and countries. And part of building a more diverse world is learning about those norms and doing what we can to navigate those in ways that help others feel comfortable and accepted.

This is especially an important skill for kids who didn't grow up with these kinds of cultural norms. Faith's kids didn't. They grew up with an Indigenous value system. That you don't make eye contact with adults because it's disrespectful. So handshake lessons were a really important thing, especially for her son. They made a game out of it, called Act Like a White Dude (seriously!). He even practiced it with his therapist, a lovely older gentleman who had also lost his father as a teenager, and knew how navigating adolescence without that can be so difficult. Honestly, this was part of a bigger lesson about how to code switch from expectations in one setting to expectations in another.

An entire book could be (and many have been) written about code-switching. It's something that most of us do naturally (though it is clearly far more difficult for individuals on the autism spectrum, those who have a social communication disorder, etc.). The idea is a simple one. We behave differently based on our surroundings (people, places, situations). This seems counterintuitive to the message of, "Be who you are!" but we are *all* multifaceted people. No one is saying to be inauthentic. Or a suck-up. Whether we like it or not, all situations have rules of engagement, both written and unwritten. Being able to move from situation to situation and navigate them effectively requires a read on what's going on and what is expected of you in the process. Effective code-switching allows you to get your wants and needs met within any situation you encounter.

# CONCLUSION

*L*isten, we've covered a lot of ground in these pages. We know you don't need all this advice like, *right now right now*, but we hope that what we've discussed will be helpful when you do need it. We like to think of this book as being a touchstone for you, a place you can turn when your kid is like, "Hey, I have this big huge life question, and let's talk about it!" For the times when you aren't sure what to say or where to start, and your heart feels like a hummingbird in your chest. For the times when you know, "This is the important shit, and I don't want to fuck it up royally, just minimally!"

In the process, we hope you recognize the main takeaways of (1) knowing yourself, (2) doing your best to have integrity for yourself and in your beliefs, and (3) aiming to be open and authentic in your tough conversations with your kids. We are all doing the best we can with the tools we have. We hope this book has given you some new tools to connect meaningfully with your kids as we wander around in the deep weeds of this complicated life.

Parenting can be hard. The world can be hard. Raising good kids in a tough world can be hard. And it can all feel thankless and unforgiving. Those feelings sometimes drive us into behaviors and spaces that ultimately are bad for us. By focusing on kindness, compassion, and self-care, you make the world a better place as a parent. This focus can give you more energy for the people and causes who need you and that you feel passionate about. The world needs your singular, beautiful energy; feed your fire with love for yourself.

# RESOURCES
# AND
# FURTHER
# READING

---

# For Parents and Kids of a Variety of Ages

*Rad Dad* (formerly a zine written by Tomas Moniz, now an anthology published by Microcosm and PM Press and edited by Moniz and Jeremy Adam Smith)

*East Village Inky* (still in print, Ayun Halliday* has an Etsy shop for subscriptions and back issues)

*And Baby Makes More: Known Donors, Queer Parents, and Our Unexpected Families* by Susan Goldberg et al.

PM Press in general publishes a *ton* on radical parenting, and they have killer deals when you order directly from them, like 50 percent–off sales pretty regularly. Because Jeff Bezos doesn't need our money.

AMightyGirl.com is an extensive collection of diverse media for all age groups.

Look for social media pages for minority-owned businesses in your area or ones that will ship to you. For example, San Antonio–Austin has a Facebook group for Black-owned businesses called For the Culture that is mostly restaurants and catering. Social Distance Powwow Marketplace, also on Facebook, is all handmade goods by Indigenous makers in Turtle Island (the United States and Canada).

*Trauma-Proofing Your Kids: A Parents' Guide for Instilling Confidence, Joy, and Resilience* by Peter Levine, PhD, and Maggie Kline

Books by Tim Tingle* for children, youth, and adults on both earlier and modern Indigenous culture (focusing mostly on Choctaw culture)

*The Trans Generation: How Trans Kids (and Their Parents) Are Creating a Gender Revolution* by Travers

*Tear Soup: A Recipe for Healing after Loss* by Pat Schwiebert and Chuck DeKlyen

*I Love My Queer Kid: A Workbook to Affirm and Support Your LGBTQ+ Child or Teen* by Marc Campbell, LMHC

*Trans Bodies/Trans Selves* (second edition) edited by Laura Erickson-Schroth

# For Older Kids and Parents

*The Cooking Gene* by Michael Twitty*

Young reader's versions of both Howard Zinn's *A People's History of the United States* and Roxanne Dunbar-Ortiz's *An Indigenous Peoples' History of the United States* (adapted by Dr. Jean Mendoza and Dr. Deb Reese*)

*Unstoppable Us: Why the World Isn't Fair* by Yuval Noah Harari

*The New Girl* by Cassandra Calin

*Go with the Flow* by Karen Schneemann

*It's Perfectly Normal: Changing Bodies, Growing Up, Sex, and Sexual Health* by Robie Harris

*Welcome to Your Period: Your Complete, No-Nonsense Guide to Going with the Flow* by Yumi Stynes and Dr. Melissa Kang

*Being You: The Body Image Book for Boys* by Charlotte Markey, Daniel Hart, and Douglas N. Zacher

*Growing Up Great: The Ultimate Puberty Book for Boys* by Scott Todnem

*The Book of Radical Answers: Real Questions from Real Kids Just Like You* by Sonya Renee Taylor

*Tiny Beautiful Things* by Cheryl Strayed

*So You Want to Talk About Race* by Ijeoma Oluo

*Uncomfortable Conversations with a Black Man* by Emmanuel Acho

*How to Be an Anti-Racist* by Ibram X. Kendi (has a self-guided journal out now too)

*Bad Feminist: Essays* by Roxane Gay

Renée Watson's books for youth and teens, *Some Places More Than Others* and *Watch Us Rise* (written with Ellen Hagan) are probably Faith's faves.

Tribal Nations Maps by Aaron Carapella* (TribalNationsMaps.com)

*The Body Is Not an Apology* by Sonya Renee Taylor

*How the Word Is Passed: A Reckoning with the History of Slavery Across America* by Dr. Clint Smith

*The Poet X* by Elizabeth Acevedo

*Felix Ever After* by Kacen Callender

*I Wish You All The Best* by Mason Deaver

*Cemetery Boys* by Aiden Thomas

*Pet* by Akwaeke Emezi

# For Younger Children

*A Day in the Life of Marlon Bundo* by Jill Twiss

*A Is for Activist* by Innosanto Nagara

*I Am Jazz* by Jessica Herthel and Jazz Jennings

*Inside Out* (great characterization of emotions, Dr. John Schinnerer* was a consultant on this Pixar film).

*My New Daddy* by Lilly Mossiano

*My New Mommy* by Lilly Mossiano

*Red: A Crayon's Story* by Michael Hall

*Sometimes Mommy Gets Angry* by Bebe Moore Campbell

*Sparkle Boy* by Lesléa Newman

   * All people with an asterisk by their name are people Faith knows either slightly through social media or is an irl friend of hers.

# ABOUT THE AUTHORS

Dr. Faith G. Harper, ACS, ACN, is a bad-ass, funny lady with a PhD. She's a licensed professional counselor, board supervisor, certified sexologist, and applied clinical nutritionist with a private practice and consulting business in San Antonio, TX. She has been an adjunct professor and a TEDx presenter, and proudly identifies as a woman of color and uppity intersectional feminist. She is the author of the book *Unf\*ck Your Brain* and many other popular zines and books on subjects such as anxiety, depression, and grief. She is available as a public speaker and for corporate and clinical trainings.

Bonnie Scott, MA, LPC-S, is a professional therapist in private practice in San Antonio, TX. Born and raised in Texas and New Mexico, she is a staunch ally to the LGBTQ community and sits on the Board of Directors for Thrive Youth Center, an emergency shelter and housing program for LGBT youth in Texas. She works hard to be an intersectional feminist, generally striving to stir up good trouble in the world. She is passionate about her kid, her cats, her books, and her profession.

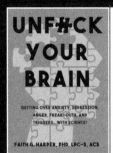

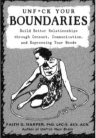